'An absolutely wonderful book.' Deborah Moggach

'Educational, entertaining, moving' *Scotsman*

'Clanchy's book says something important about female refugees, who are often as much in flight from aspects of their old life as persecution. Male immigrants dominate the news, but there are many women like Antigona in Western Europe, doing their best for their children and living in constant fear that their efforts won't be enough . . .

[T]he book is a tribute to their friendship. But it is also about the vulnerability of marginal women, of whom Antigona's fate is tragically emblematic.'

Joan Smith, *Sunday Times*

'The portrait of a brilliant, violent Albanian family torn from its rocky roots is only half the point . . . what Clanchy learns about herself, about her country and the way it treats those who seek protection – all of this is as painful, flawed and true as what she learns about Antigona and Albania.

Clanchy is a poet, and this is a poets' book, earthily written and packed with precise imagery . . . a scholarly book, well-researched and accurate, and not least a political book, which asks if we properly value mother-love, and how we can change the balance between rich and poor.' Carole Angier, *Independent*

'Clanchy's is a set of eyes we can trust. Her struggle to understand Antigona's abusive husband mirrors our own, and her richly suggestive language, revealing her background, brings sinister undertones to the women who gather to inspect the bridal bedsheets and read "sentence of the stain." Such a Western female perspective makes this more than a "refugee"'s story. It becomes instead a narrative of convergence; an exploration of being female, of cultural conditioning and, most importantly, of sisterhood.' *New Statesman*

'Clanchy has an eye for detail and a good ear for dialogue – part of her poet's training. But in this long-form writing style which is for her a new departure she displays a wonderful feel for narrative nuance' *Sunday Telegraph*

'Remarkably lucid' *Evening Standard*

Antigona and Me

Also by Kate Clanchy

Slattern
Samarkand
Newborn
All the Poems You Need to Say Hello (ed.)

Antigona and Me

KATE CLANCHY

PICADOR

First published 2008 by Picador as *What Is She Doing Here?*

First published in paperback 2009 by Picador
an imprint of Pan Macmillan Ltd
Pan Macmillan, 20 New Wharf Road, London N1 9RR
Basingstoke and Oxford
Associated companies throughout the world
www.panmacmillan.com

ISBN 978-0-330-44933-5

1 3 5 7 9 8 6 4 2

A CIP catalogue record for this book is available
from the British Library.

Printed and bound in the UK by
CPI Mackays, Chatham ME5 8TD

For the real Antigona,
and the women behind her.

Contents

Preface 1
1 The Kosovan Woman 9
2 Highlanders 22
3 Dirty, Clean, and the Kanun of Lek 60
4 How She Left Him 94
5 Pastoral: A Collection of All the Other Things Antigona Knows How to Do and I Don't 113
6 The Mountain Woman, the Pasha's Wife, and the Problem 129
7 Nannies, Maids, and *The Revenger's Tragedy* 147
8 Albanian Stories 169
9 Who Do They Think They Are? 206
10 Your Nanny, Your Mum 250
Epilogue: Flora's CV 269

Select Bibliography 273
Acknowledgements 274

PREFACE

Spring 2005, London Fields. I am walking across the park with Antigona, a baby, and a toddler. I'm going somewhere: I'm wearing my good coat, carrying my briefcase, heading for the station. Antigona is in nanny mode: pushchair, cut-offs, hi-tops. Nanny is one of the things she is to me: also neighbour, protégée, cleaner, confidante, and friend. Something struggles in the grass near the road, flutters a grey wing – a feral pigeon, surely, bashed by a bus. I look away – sick animals scare me – but Antigona darts forward, picks the bird up by the briefly fanned pinion, and folds it into her hands. A light stripe flashes at its neck: a wood pigeon, I realize with a pang, one of the sweet plump creatures which sometimes ornament the London plane trees and send their deep rural coos through the blare of the traffic.

Soft matter falls from the bird. Antigona holds it deftly clear, then walks over to show me: the dove has died in her cupped hands, its eyes shut, its beak slightly bloody and meekly bent on its soft pink breast, a perfect little martyr. 'He gave up just like a person,' she says wonderingly. And then: 'Just like my cousin.'

'In the War?' I ask. Antigona is a refugee of the 1999 Kosovan War.

'No,' she says. 'Just in his bed. I was child. I went to help my aunty, my Mum send me. My cousin is in bed, long time sick, breathing like that, like the bird.'

'Struggling?'

'Yes. And I go in, take his hand, and he give up. Just like that.'

Antigona lays the body tenderly in a clump of dock leaves. 'So he can get better,' she tells the toddler, who is anxious, 'get mended.' And she invites her to 'chase Nanny', and, after a few skirmishes round the push-chair, returns to the conversation she'd been haranguing me with previously, in which I was trying and failing to explain why I prefer not to shop at Primark. The whole incident – the countrywoman's skill with which she picked up the bird, the elemental grace with which she gave the creature its death, the vignette of her lost country, the spin back to the twenty-first-century consumer culture which she has so wholeheartedly adopted, the sublime and the banal effortlessly juxtaposed – is utterly typical of her. 'When I get back,' I think, and it is a familiar, almost weary thought, 'I'll have to write it down.'

For I had been writing about Antigona for years, by then – ever since I met her, in fact, back in 2001. As I'd got to know her, I'd also read books on Kosovo and asked her questions about them – almost as if I were conducting research. In fact, since the new baby, this seemed to be the only writing I was actually completing. Some of my early notes had grown into something like short stories; others were dated lists or bald accounts of library forays interspersed with *Antigona Quotes* in italic; still others were pages of dialogue, like sketches for radio plays. However much I wrote, I still had the harassing sense of falling behind, of missing the best bits, because at that time Antigona seemed to be telling me her life in vast chunks, filling my helpless ears with horrors like Coleridge's Wedding-Guest's. And her story wouldn't stop: some particularly dramatic incidents had actually, recently, occurred in my kitchen. It was becoming, I thought as I stood on the station platform, a problem. Perhaps I should stop listening to Antigona, recover my voice and write another book of poetry. Unless I was writing a book already. In which case, I should probably stop *that*. After all, I didn't write prose, and this wasn't my life, and Antigona was my employee.

No: 'employee' was wrong. That sounded as if I had a company, she a desk. Antigona cleared up for me, she put the baby on the breast for me, she scraped the shit off the nappies for me: Antigona was my servant, and just thinking the word, let alone admitting it in print, made me burn with shame. I was supposed to be a liberal, a feminist, not an oppressive overlord. And even if I followed the advice I always gave out at Creative Writing classes – 'write the thing you are most ashamed of, because that is where the interest lies' – it seemed hardly fair to do so on Antigona's, rather than my own, behalf. I had power over Antigona: I paid her and wrote her references. What is more, I had thirty-nine years of speaking English and eighteen years of studying it to her tenuous five. She would never be able to control my medium of literature, and it seemed like another kind of servitude to conscript her into it, to steal her plot for its drama and colour: it seemed like appropriation, which is a polite word for theft.

These were the reasons, I supposed, why I had never developed my *Antigona* files into anything I wanted to publish. Yet her story compelled me, and it wasn't just the drama; it was because it seemed resonant, representative. When I read the news, or caught discussions on the radio, or talked to friends, I found myself thinking of Antigona, quoting her, telling a tale from her life to illustrate my point, whether about feminism or immigration or Eastern Europe or Tony Blair. Hers was the voice which was missing from these discussions, from our public discourse, hers and the voice of many exploited immigrants, especially women: I felt that more and more strongly. I knew Antigona thought that too, and that she had, moreover, a strong sense of herself as a special person, a pioneer, someone of destiny. Perhaps she might want to be memorialized. She would certainly, I reminded myself, have a view on the matter, because she has views on everything. Just because she has never read a book in English doesn't mean she does not know that books are powerful things. I should ask. So I did, a few days later, when she had just finished filling in the details of one of her great escapes.

'How would you feel if I wrote your life down, Antigona? Like, in a book?'

'Good,' she said at once, as if she had already thought

of it. 'Good. And then a feature film, actually. Mini-series.'

I said I didn't think I could deliver on the feature film front, but that I thought her story was very interesting and exciting and—

'Yes,' she said. 'It makes me feel happy – a book. It makes me feel relaxed. For me. And because there are a thousand women behind me in this country, having shit lives, 'scuse my language. No one can understand their lives, here. They are stuck, they cannot move forward. It takes one to break the ice.'

'Break the ice' has always suggested to me a thin frozen layer over faces at a party: something, like the gloss on crème brûlée, to be cracked with a toffee hammer. Now, in Antigona's brilliant inversion, I saw that the ice for her was thick: opaque, grey lake ice, and she and the other women were under it, knocking. If she broke through, a torrent would follow.

I didn't think I could write anything that would have any such dramatic effect. Nor could I turn out the sensational novelization which I suspected Antigona had in mind: I couldn't pretend to imagine being her, because one of the things she had taught me was that our two cultures had made us profoundly, not superficially, different. I was starting to think of another book, a book about that difference. Not Antigona's story as it happened to her, but her story as it happened to me: as I heard it, as I researched it and imagined it; as it made me think; as it changed me. I would put myself in the book as I was and am: me with all my ignorances and prejudices and losses of temper, me with my large, British, liberal behind, and the reader would have to consciously peer past me, would never be allowed to forget that this was a particular, partial view of a life, not a life itself. In the house, in our conversations, Antigona and I were always equals, shocking and irritating each other with our differences, certainly, but never losing our sense of closeness: the feeling that in one another, we had met our equivalent, our match. I would write about that exchange.

'Because I never think – you know – what I want to say in the book, is that you and I know different things, but I never think you are stupider than me, ever,' I blurted out to Antigona. She went pink, her jaw tightened, and she nodded.

'You have the right feeling for me. You will write the right thing. Stop worrying,' she said.

Antigona's absolute trust in me made some things easier, and some harder. The issues of what to include and what to censor were actually relatively easy to decide: I simply asked Antigona, in person or on the phone, what she thought about a particular issue or incident, and then read out or summarized – because Antigona is often baffled by my written register, and bored, let's be honest, with my philosophizing – what I was writing to make sure she was content. But I was much less sanguine than Antigona about her privacy: I could see harm coming to her from the book, from her own community above all, but also from the media and even from the law. So, from the beginning, I changed all names and all locations, and further protected the identities of members of her family by altering ages and degrees of kinship and by using composite characters. This was made easier for me when some of the principal actors in the story coincidentally left the country. No character in this book should now be identified with any particular person of Kosovan origin currently living in the UK.

Nevertheless, Antigona and I wanted, from the outset, for the book to be as truthful as possible, and in this cause I have stuck as closely as possible to the facts as they appeared to me, while still maintaining Antigona's disguise. I have actually invented only a few sentences of this text, but I have occasionally transposed or edited narratives, always down a key, making the plot line less, not more, sensational. There must be other inventions here, though, of which I am not aware, because all the stories in this book are told and retold, by Antigona, by me, by Antigona's relatives, and sometimes by third or fourth parties. Sometimes I also present facts which I have learned from books or articles: these are not intended to be fictions and any errors are mine. The copyright is mine too, but I nevertheless regard this as a shared text. I have already paid to Antigona more than I have received in advance for this book, and if the book goes on to make more money, then I shall tithe it to her and to her children. I am still constantly in touch with all of them, and very much aware of their needs.

That day in London Fields, I watched Antigona from the high station platform, strolling at toddler pace across the park, and was struck by how ordinary she suddenly looked, in the same way that her feline beauty falls away from her in photographs, where she often appears small, shrunken-cheeked, scowling. No one will notice her, I thought, as she stooped to pick up the little one from a tumble, except perhaps to wonder idly if she is Brazilian or Italian; no one will look twice at an immigrant woman with a pushchair of blond children, a mobile phone flashing at her ear. It is only I and the children who saw her don the guise of the Goddess Isis, giver of life and death, and doff it again, easily as rubber gloves; it is only we who witnessed her encapsulate, in a gesture, the beauty and violence and tenderness of another, rapidly disappearing, way of life. That act was not on any record, nor were most of the extraordinary acts of her extraordinary life: she was, at best, a statistic. I knew her as much more. If I took the path of ignoring the story I had been given, of suppressing that vision, I would be joining the crowds who walked past her. But if I wanted, instead, I could go home and start writing it down.

I

The Kosovan Woman

No one in the West who has seen what is happening in Kosovo can doubt that NATO's military action is justified. Bismarck famously said the Balkans were not worth the bones of one Pomeranian Grenadier. Anyone who has seen the tear-stained faces of the hundreds of thousands of refugees streaming across the border, heard their heart-rending tales of cruelty or contemplated the unknown fates of those left behind, knows that Bismarck was wrong.

Tony Blair, April 1999

'Where are they from, that family?' said my husband one afternoon in early 2001. Spring: we had the front window open. 'I keep seeing them in the street. Like Italians, but they're not speaking Italian. That's not Greek, is it?'

I peered out. A young woman, two girls – early teenagers with long plaits of hair – and a round-eyed little boy were filling the pavement with their clamour. I'd often seen them before. Once, mother and daughters had come screaming down the street, wailing and keening, the little boy slung like luggage over his mother's shoulder. 'I think,' I said, remembering recent newscasts, 'I think they might be from the former Yugoslavia.'

'Haven't they all gone home?'

'Not if they can help it, I shouldn't think.'

A few days later, I meet the woman and her son in the street. The little boy is carrying a yellow balloon with 'Liberal Democrat' on it. In seconds, he has presented it to my toddling baby, and is hugging and kissing him. The woman squats down and hugs the baby too. It is his blondness, I think, that excites these effusions, his *non Angli sed angeli*. It reminds me of being on family holidays in Italy in the seventies, when my similarly golden-haired brother would be clasped to upholstered black bosoms until he fainted.

Not that this woman is upholstered. She is spry, elegant, quick, and the pony tail of black hair down her back is magnificently shiny and alive. She raises her head to look at me. A beautiful face: the poise and proportions and kholed dark eyes of a cheetah. She jumps up, and I see we are going to talk.

'Are you from Yugoslavia?'

'Kosovo.'

'Ah.' I make a warm, generally approving noise. 'Three children?'

'Yes. You one?'

'Just one.' She picks up my hand. She is looking for a wedding ring, I realize. I show her, expecting the sort of cloying moral congratulations, the sort of glad-handing that used to embarrass me in Kashmir or Anatolia, but instead she shows me her own hands. They are worn, brown, strong, with pronounced knuckles – and bare.

'I am dee-vorced,' she says, and looks closely at me, scanning my face for disapproval. 'Dee-vorced. He beat me up.'

'Good,' I say. 'Good. I'm sure that's a good idea.' She smiles, and I see that all her teeth are false.

Her little boy is chasing my little boy, three steps forward, three steps back. He is extraordinarily good at it, extraordinarily interested in the younger child. The baby giggles: that pure, bubbling, rippling sound. We lean against a low wall, the Kosovan woman and I, relax in the early spring sun. She tells me her name: Antigona, four long syllables, with the stress on the 'go'. I tell her mine. I have the feeling, at least in my memory, of strongly meeting someone, of making an important connection. And I have an idea.

'Do you want a job?' I say.

'Are you sure that will be all right?' says my husband, when I announce that someone for whom we have no references and whose second name we do not know will, for the foreseeable future, be working as our cleaner and be a keyholder in our household.

'Yeah,' I say. 'Honestly. She's great. I trust her. It's a woman thing. And we really need help in the house. We agreed.'

And when he raises his eyebrows, indicating that not only am I being irrational but probably – typically, self-destructively, sentimentally – am about to get *over-involved, again* (I once adopted a kitten with fleas, worms and leukaemia, and it was not me who administered the pills, nor took it on its final journey to the vet), I say:

'Come on. She's from *Kosovo*. She ran away from the *Serbs*. We have to trust her.'

I am calling on a mutual soft spot, an area of warm agreement we share not only with everyone we know, but with many people we usually disagree with, such as the voters of Middle America, and the leader writers of the *Daily Mail*. We know, we think, what *Kosovo* means: green hills, burnt-out villages, vast convoys of refugees on tractors. I remember that high-tech control room; NATO spokesman Jamie Shea dominating newscasts, telling us that perhaps 100,000 Albanians were in mass graves; Tony Blair receiving the adoration of camp-loads of refugees. We know what Kosovo was like: like Bosnia, wasn't it? Dark-eyed Muslims from the Balkans, suffering, on mountains. But not as bad, because this time Blair and Clinton had started talking the kind of language we approved of, about individuals and ethics. This time we had helped, this time we had run the film back and done it differently. This time we had sent in the good soldiers – albeit all of them in aeroplanes, which concerned me at the time – before all the villages were torched, before the young men were herded like cattle to the killing field.

Even Mark, our builder – in this book I am nearly always doing up one or another early Victorian house in Hackney – is pro-Kosovar. His Polish father, dark skin, wide travels and warm intelligence do not usually prevent him from expressing the view that all refugees are Social Security scroungers out to take our jobs. But he makes an exception here, and not just because Antigona, on only her second day at work in my house, has hijacked the espresso-maker and made him a coffee with boiled milk and three sugars. 'She's from Kosovo, ain't she?' he says. 'I don't object to that. They had no choice, with them Serbs. They had to come here.' And he looks over to Antigona with a most peculiar expression on his face: not lust exactly, more Madonna-worship. As if her dark hair and eyes, the spring in her step, the broom in her hand, recalled an ideal of the south and womanhood deeply imprinted on his English unconscious. It's like a scene from *Il Postino*.

Though Antigona seems to take a lot of men that way. Even the lugubrious proprietor of the Italian delicatessen, the man with the vast gorgonzola neck who has never done more for me than sigh heavily over my choice of anti-pasti, has spotted us walking down the street, and asks me if I know her phone number, and offers me free apricot juice. 'Is she Italian?' he asks. 'Sardinian?'

'No,' I say. 'Kosovo. Refugee.' And watch that expression cross his face, the moue of surprise, the tender nod. 'Albanian asylum-seeker' would not, I think, have had the same effect.

'How did she get here, then?' says Mark. Midsummer. He is back for another job, and has found Antigona a fixture in the house, thoroughly comfortable with the cupboards, mistress of the washing machine. Mark approves. How she shifts, he says, how much better the whole place looks. He has already proposed marriage and been turned down. Antigona has nonetheless made him a coffee.

'She carried her wounded daughter out of a burning village on her back,' I say. And watch Mark's eyes widen and soften. 'Then she got in a lorry,' I add, seizing the moment as I know that Mark has strong views on the misuse of lorries. It's the plight of the lads driving that gets him. 'Well,' says Mark, gulping coffee, 'of course. In the circumstances. You would. '

I let him have the whole story, in fact, seeing as I have it. The day after I met Antigona in the street, I put a note through her door, asking her to come by. She came, rather dressed up, with both her teenage daughters and the little boy Ylli holding her hand. I offered tea, and made it, and nobody drank it. I felt awkward, but the girls curled up like cats on my new fluffy rug and petted my baby, covering him with kisses, making him walk with his little trolley. One was darker, taller, stronger, one very thin and pale; both had glossy hair and fringed eyes like colts. I had no idea which was older.

Meanwhile, Antigona cased the joint: walking up and down the stairs, checking my cleaning cupboard, the state of all the rooms. She spoke to her daughters. The darker one said, 'I am Mihane. My mum will take the job. Eight pounds an hour. Four hours a week. But you will find her other jobs.' I knew that would be easy, so I agreed. Then, almost as another item of business, Mihane told me, as she had clearly often told before, the outline of their escape from Kosovo. Antigona has added many details since, and Flora, the paler and, it turns out, older daughter has been round for some help with her homework and filled in her part. Flora's poised, elegant English is really remarkable for someone who has only been in the country a year, but she clearly gets her storytelling ability from her mother. Both tell a tale with tremendous immediacy, a terrific mixture of detail and restraint, their slim arms shaking, their dark, liquid eyes apparently fixed on the scene.

The Serbs came for Antigona in March '99. Four policemen, heavily armed, arrived looking for Fazli, Antigona's husband – ex-husband, I teach her to say, since she is divorced, and she does, often, with relish – who they maintained had Kosovan Liberation Army information. Antigona said she hadn't seen him for a long while, which was perfectly true, but the Serbs didn't believe her. One policeman held Antigona, Mihane (ten), and Ylli (two) at gunpoint in the kitchen, and the others dragged Flora, who was just thirteen, onto the flat roof of the house.

The policemen called out to Fazli in the dark fields and terraces, the forest beyond, told him that they had his daughter and would drop her off the two-storeyed building. They told Flora to call out and she did, knowing all the time that her father was not there. Flora says she found herself thinking not so much of herself but of her baby brother. Ylli's life – it is the family oath. Ylli, his soft round head and wondering eyes; Ylli on his mother's lap; Ylli's pretty plump hands reaching out to the barrel of a gun. They told her to scream and she found that quite easy. She screamed and screamed and Fazli did not come and after a while they threw her off the roof – one with her hands, one with her feet, like the bumps at a birthday party – and then they went home. They did not, on this occasion, shoot the baby.

Flora still carries the wound in her hip – the bone was cracked and is now slightly deformed and gives her a good deal of trouble. At the time, she could do nothing but lie on her side and breathe painfully. Antigona could get no medical help for her, not even painkillers. The village was paralysed, waiting. The Serbs came back a few nights later. The village trailed down a high valley, smallholding by smallholding; Antigona's house was near the top. She saw the smoke billowing upwards from the bottom of the valley, and ran to wake the children. She took Flora on her back. Mihane carried Ylli. They ran through the door and did not look back. Antigona has never seen or heard of any of her husband's family since that hour: the mother, brother and two sister-in-laws with whom she had been living cheek by jowl for fourteen years. They left everything behind: furniture, livestock, the ends of crops painfully harvested the previous autumn, seeds for the coming year, pots, pans, clothes. And a dog, Ylli says. A dog he really liked and who liked him.

They were in the forest all night. The next day they got to a neighbouring village where Antigona cashed in a favour and they got a lift higher up the mountains. From here, over many days, carrying Flora, getting lifts, sleeping in the woods, they reached Fazli's cousin's house near the Albanian border. Fazli had got on a boat to Puglia, they heard, but no one knew if he had landed. Weeks passed, months; no sign of Fazli, no money, not much to eat. Refugees trailed through the village on the road to Albania. Antigona could find out nothing of her own family, though she heard many stories of atrocities in their area. Maybe they had got out in time, over the hills into Macedonia; maybe not.

The cousin was kind, but Fazli was still missing and resources were limited. In the end, Antigona gave the cousin all her money and he took her somewhere she could get on a lorry. For three days, or perhaps longer – it was difficult to tell – they were rattled around in the back. It was very cold, so Antigona took off her coat and wrapped up the small Ylli between her knees. They had to keep shushing him. It was dark; it was a very long way. They slept.

Years later, during one of my son's recurrent train fixations, Antigona was astonished to learn that a railway goes under the English Channel. As Sam prattled on about the many merits of the Eurostar, she said, dazed, 'I thought we were on a train. When we were on the lorry. But I knew England was over the sea and I did not see how it could be.'

The lorry disgorges them at dawn just outside Gravesend. They stand in the road, and the tiny, round-eyed Ylli, then, as now, an enormously appealing child, sticks out a thumb. A car stops and a man looks them up and down. 'Kosovo,' says Antigona, and he motions them to get in. He drives them to the train station and buys tickets to Victoria, walks them to the platform, gives them a piece of paper with an address, and shows them which train to get on.

At Victoria they get off and look. Antigona makes several false starts, then grabs the arm of a middle-aged city gent, gesturing for directions to the address on the piece of paper. The gent thinks for a moment – he must have thought they were Roma, at first. 'Kosovo,' says Antigona again, indicating her little tableau of children, hollow-eyed under the Christmas lights. The gent puts them in a four-square London taxi, and gives the driver a twenty-pound note. The piece of paper turns out to be the address of our local church, where our lefty vicar has turned most of his crumbling Gothic pile into a refugee centre. Kind people take the little family to Social Services, where the children fall asleep on the delightfully warm carpet. Antigona tells her story, desperate, animated and compelling. Flora fills in with the Serbs and the roof. Ylli raises his big eyes to the social workers and gives his beautiful smile. Of course, they get asylum. Even Mark, who, when I get to this point in the story, has his head down and is mopping his face with his bandana, would have given them asylum.

Antigona retells the end of the story every year, at Christmas time. Social Services assign them a room and give them some money and a church person takes Antigona to Tesco, where she is deeply impressed by the range of unseasonal produce. The next day, the family wakes up warm, safe, fed. It is Christmas morning, the traffic is hushed, and the frosty air is saturated with bells: the bells of the buried London villages, sounding out the parish boundaries. Oranges and Lemons; the Old Bailey calling in her debts; Shoreditch and Stepney still hoping to grow rich, all these centuries on. Antigona and her family gaze out of the window at families slithering down the pavements, waving their new hats and gloves, taking the Christmas bike for a spin. 'I did feel really grateful,' says Antigona. 'Really glad of this country.'

After I have known Antigona perhaps six weeks, she tells me a story for herself. It comes to me slowly, through her halting English and my suggestions, like a film run too slowly, frame by crackling frame.

Antigona is cleaning the kitchen and I am playing with the baby. Again, she wonders at the child's golden hair. Sam won't grow up blond, I say, not when I'm so dark; just look at his eyelashes. I love his eyelashes, dark as mascara, the very length and curve of a Disney creature's.

Antigona wipes the stove. She says I must stop rejoicing in the baby's eyelashes or I will invoke the envy of neighbours, which will in turn bring down the power of the Bad Eye. The Evil Eye? I say, remembering an amulet I had as a child, a coral horn on a charm bracelet. Yes.

Antigona's own younger sister was blonde, she says. And not just in Sam's tow-headed way, either, nor as Ylli, she maintains, was once light-haired. No. Antigona's younger sister had blue eyes, which is vanishingly rare in Kosovo and much, much to be admired. Also her blonde hair curled. Also she is dead.

And this is how she died. Antigona's mother, who had by then five children, fell terribly ill. She was a valuable person in the family because she looked after not only all of them but also the family smallholding, so Antigona's aunts, her mother's sisters, decided to save her. They went to – the Imam? Not exactly. More like the magic man, but he is definitely using the Koran and he is definitely, definitely real, true: he has magic. The Magic Man says that Antigona's mother is under a curse and must die. The aunts must buy magic papers.

'Do you believe that?' I ask.

I don't. I don't believe this. This does not belong in my world, this glimpse under the flap of an Ottoman tent, this pile of rugs, this magic-dealing holy man. It is as if I had opened one of my nice Ikea cabinets and discovered a freshly sacrificed goat. Antigona is my contemporary, she is from Europe, and I want her, at this point, to tell me of course this is a con trick, a load of hooey.

But no. She is adamant. The magic papers were real, were true, were magic. I should watch out for curses, they are everywhere. The Magic Man wrote the magic sentence down on paper, and folded the paper, and gave it to the aunties, like an amulet, and that was how the magic started. The rule of the magic papers was: they would let one person back across Lethe, but only if another body were given in exchange. The only way to save Antigona's mother was to sacrifice another member of the family. The aunts nominated the blonde baby, and put the papers in her cot, and, within days, the baby, who had been perfectly healthy, died, and the mother recovered. Antigona remembers it well.

She didn't know about the papers and the magic exchange, though, until she was thirty and her aunt came to visit and told her that it had been a near thing between the baby and Antigona. The blonde curls had been narrowly outweighed by Antigona's already evident sprightly health and capacity for work. A mistake, of course. Had they known that Antigona would marry Fazli and be beaten up so very regularly, they'd definitely have chosen her. It would have been a blessing to her.

I begin to understand what this story is about. It is not a horror story, though I am horrified: it is about the worth of Antigona's life. It is another version of 'I am dee-vorced, dee-vorced,' and the out-held bare hand.

'What did you say to that?' I ask, gently now.

'I didn't say anything,' says Antigona, 'because my aunty didn't know I was going to come here and have my life here.'

'Your life here is hard.'

'No. You don't know, Kate, the difference my life there and my life here. There I was like a dog. I borrowed money for bread. Here – I can work. I can do anything. I can choose my life.'

'So you were the right one to save?'

'Yeah. Now I am the lucky one.' And Antigona thinks some more about her aunty.

'Bitch,' says Antigona thoughtfully, polishing the stove top to a sheen. Her English is coming along in leaps and bounds.

2

Highlanders

Things Antigona Knows How to Do and I Don't: No. 1

MOPPING (APPARENTLY)

I do mop, just not very often and with a squeegee. The first time she comes to my house, as a condition of taking the job, Antigona says I must go out and buy a cotton mop and mop bucket, so I do.

The first day she comes to work for me, she hauls all the chairs on top of the kitchen table. She drags the rugs out to the garden and beats them on the line with a broom handle. She vacuums the entire floor for a full twenty minutes. Then she mops, squeezing the cotton mop till it is almost dry, pressing and lifting all the dirt off the floor. The lino shines, and she turns to me and smiles.

She smells of sweat. I don't. Her eyes gleam with triumph.

'I'm strong,' she says. 'You are not.'

Things I Know How to Do and Antigona Doesn't: No. 1

Write to the Council, once a week, with a list of the faults in Antigona's hostel, enclosing photos, doctors' notes and taped-on mouse droppings, until the accommodation is changed. In the new place, get all the basic services working by phoning up lots of call centres from my landline. Use my credit card to get the electricity charged to a meter instead of the cruelly expensive 'key' system. Write letters to the Council pointing out that Antigona is entitled to Single Person's Allowance on her Council Tax. Phone up the Council serially, over a number of days, until I get hold of the right official capable of actually registering this change on the computer. Reply to cryptic missives from the Home Office, getting all the reference numbers in the right places.

I know how to, so I do. I become Antigona's chief employer, scribe and confidante and this happens rapidly, within three months. I make all the running: it becomes one of my projects. Why are you doing all that, says my husband, isn't it taking a lot of Your Time. Because, since we had the baby, I am always banging on about My Time, and how I have none any more, and taking on a cleaner was supposed to make some extra. I invent some answers.

I am doing this because: living where I live, I am often confronted with the barriers language puts in front of immigrants, often see small and large humiliations visited on people all too aware of what is happening to them. Every refugee, I think, even a fluent English speaker, even one with an advanced degree, needs an amanuensis. Language and letters are easy for me, and I had been vaguely intending to volunteer to take English classes, or for Citizen's Advice, but never got round to it: so helping Antigona saves me the trouble.

I am doing this because: Antigona is a fantastic cleaner, hasn't he noticed? She has energy, she has initiative, she is not frightened to delve to the bottom of the wash heap, or to tackle the no-go area under the stairs. Our house is orderly now, clean; it has a rhythm of tidying and straightening. She saves loads of My Time – not just the four hours per week cleaning, but the numberless hours I previously spent staring at the cleaning and feeling bad about it.

I am doing this because: I like Antigona. She is vigorous, she is illuminating, she is funny. Her causes are my sort of causes. I wouldn't do it, for example, for her husband.

Mostly, though, I am doing this because: having someone clean my house makes me feel powerfully guilty and obliged. When I am typing upstairs, 'working' on something as small and commercially insignificant as a poem, and Antigona is cleaning downstairs, each bang of the broom makes me blush. I shut the door, but even then I find myself hopping about the room, chewing my fingers. I seek out journalism to do on Antigona's days, because a short deadline and swift cheque make me feel more useful. To be honest, the letters seem a small undertaking, compared to the mopping. If we do it this way, if I spend at least half an hour of her four hours discussing her life over one of her coffees, I can manage to have her in my house without doing something irrational, such as crying, and begging for another go with the mop.

There were staging posts, though, to intimacy.

Just a couple of weeks after we met, there was the crisis of the sweet factory. Antigona had a job there, on the production line. She told me that the sweet factory man wanted her papers, her numbers; and I, with visions of sweatshops and gangmasters, told her to quit at once. Yes, she said, but I must then find her more cleaning jobs. She was already fixed up with some of my friends, but I said a notice in the Deli was the thing, and I wrote her one, quoting my phone number and reference, and within days she was fully booked.

Then there were various incidents with Fazli, the Ex-Husband. Antigona had thrown him out months before she met me; her divorce was almost complete, but he was still very much in the country: following her from job to job, leering at her outfits, racing her to Ylli's school to pick the child up and insult the teachers, menacing the girls at bus stops, driving around her house at night in a stolen car – so many things I have forgotten the order of them. I remember teaching her to ask for the right police officer on the phone, though, and to say, 'Hello, I am calling to log another incident,' and peering out of the window to see if he was there –

he was, once – and walking her back up the road to her house. 'Like *EastEnders* for you, innit,' she said one day, and she was right: I liked the drama.

I liked the raw politics of it, too. Her papers, for instance. When Antigona first arrived here, in 1999, she got a year's Exceptional Leave to Remain. As it ran out, she applied for more. The process was rather slow, and was still going on when I met her in 2001. In the autumn, it was reaching a crisis, and we went over her case together. Her lawyer was saying that not only was Kosovo still dangerous, but it was an impossible place for a divorced woman: neat feminism, just what interests me most.

Eventually, Antigona was summoned to Croydon to explain herself. Antigona is nervous about travel, and we spent a lot of time studying the map and looking up trains. But she returned triumphant. She had made her way through the maze of corridors that is Lunar House, the massive Home Office Immigration Centre; she had waited her turn on plastic chairs and duly been summoned to a carpet-tiled pod; she had managed without an interpreter; she had been heard and it would be OK. On a dark day in November 2001, Antigona turned up radiant. She had been granted four years' Leave to Remain, with Travel Documents. She could save money, she could keep her children at school, and she could go to Albania and Macedonia and look for her lost family. I liked that too, very much. I thought: my country can do this. Despite everything, we are a liberal democracy. It made me proud.

It meant more letters, though. The new papers

entitled her to go on the Council Housing List. This meant she was off the Social Services Housing List – the cosy house in my street – and into first stage council housing – two dirty rooms in a hostel with shared kitchen and bathroom – a week before Christmas. We lent a heater and sheets, and my husband moved her stuff in the car. I actually asked her for Christmas, hoping she wouldn't come, not telling my husband, but in the end she spent the entire time in Clissold Park, with some friends.

And the Hasan episode, above all. That also happened in the winter of the dirty hostel, 2001–2, another dark counterpoint to the happy story of Antigona getting her Leave to Remain. It was then that I started to phone Antigona on days when I didn't employ her, then that I started to visit her house for coffee, then that we actually became friends.

Hasan was Antigona's cousin, she said. He was also connected to the Clissold Park people and seemed to live on their sofa a lot, but Antigona's English disappeared when I tried to make out exactly what the relationships were. She worried about him because he was so depressed and on tablets and kept getting fired from jobs.

'Did he have a bad war?' I asked. I was learning this question, and getting used to accounts of men in the Kosovan community addicted to gambling, and women who tried to kill themselves in the bath. A 'bad war' is the phrase Antigona used to cover all sorts of suffering which no one wants to name: rape, torture, displacement, disgrace. The Clissold Park wife came over on the UN airlifts, I knew that, and the airlift people had always had spectacularly Bad Wars.

'Before the war,' says Antigona, 'it happened. Hasan came here '98. That's why his papers are bad.'

Any refugee from the former Yugoslavia who arrived in this country after June '99 got a year's Exceptional Leave to Remain at once. This was a special edict of Jack Straw, the Home Secretary, because, embarrassingly, the passage of Labour's new Asylum Bill through Parliament – a bill which restricted the rights of asylum-seekers, forbade them to work, and replaced benefits with vouchers – coincided exactly with the Kosovan war, the UNHCR airlifts, and Tony Blair's speech urging us all to look into the refugees' faces for righteousness. But earlier arrivals like Hasan had often been treated much more doubtfully, even though Kosovo was acknowledged to be unsafe, even though very many of them, like Hasan, were victims of torture at the hands of the Serb Police.

'Just one time,' said Antigona. 'They wanted his brother, actually. His brother he is KLA. But just a few days.'

Just a few days. A village prison. A length of flex. The Serbs in '97. 'The war,' said Antigona, 'it happens always. People think it start '98, but it happen all the time.' She had paused in her work, was staring through the countertop.

'He is boy,' she said. 'You know, he is child, really.'

Antigona is brisk about all her actions, but sometimes she stops short and seems to go somewhere else entirely, through a sort of hole in time. Antigona is scornful of retrospect, and doctors, but now and then, despite herself, the street opens and she falls through and is returned to the war, but to a different version of the war, in which, as in a bad dream, she is a paralysed observer.

One day, for instance, she came to work in a terrible state because she had seen security guards turn a homeless man out of Tesco. They threw him out, says Antigona, it made a horrible noise when he landed, he hurt his back. They laughed at him, the guards; one of them rolled him with his foot. Antigona went to shout at them, but she couldn't shout, she couldn't remember her English. Ylli was there, it was terrible. She was pointing at Ylli and crying, and she was stuck, she couldn't get past there. She went to the man and he was rolled over, looking at the gutter, and everyone was walking by. She didn't know what to do, and after a while she was still sitting there and she took the homeless man's hand, and spoke to him in Albanian.

Anyway. Hasan was just seventeen when whatever happened, happened. And when, to oblige Antigona, I hired him to move rubble out of our garden, he still seemed much younger than his twenty-two years. He was shorter than Antigona and very thin and had adenoidal breathing and a downy moustache. He took hours over the job and left a load of stone on the grass and a heap of cigarette ends in the compost heap.

'What was he doing here?' said Mark, when he saw the mess. As time had passed, his views on Kosovars had rather reverted to type. 'I hate that. She's one thing, that Anita, she's lovely. But the guy who did this is a useless git. He should go home.'

As it happened, the Home Office agreed. Late in 2001, just after Antigona got her Leave to Remain extended, Hasan's appeal for more time here was rejected. Antigona viewed this as an utter disaster. It wasn't that Hasan was having such a great time here, but he had, she explained, no home to go to. His home village had been burned and looted, and his parents and sisters and nephews and nieces had wholesale disappeared. The Red Cross had no record of them, not a single name. Yes, of course they'd asked. Many times. Maybe they were in a hole in the ground. There were massacres in that area, there were mass graves. Hasan did not want to go and look, he wanted to sit on the carpet in the house in Clissold Park and watch *Neighbours*. He made a second appeal, which, as his solicitor said, is fairly routine in these cases.

Then, suddenly, in the new year of 2002, Hasan was arrested. Antigona came to me in tears. Her panic was terrible. I had never seen her so distressed – her face taut, her eyes showing the whites, like an animal with its foot in a trap. Hasan was in the police cells and she had no idea what to do, how to visit him, give him cigarettes – did I know who to speak to? And I said that we were not in a totalitarian country and Hasan had the right to visitors, but this turned out to be quite wrong.

In a few horrifying calls, I found out that if someone is being held in a police cell by Immigration then they have no visiting hours and no rights to visitors or phone calls, except to their solicitor. But you can ring the officer on duty and wheedle, and if you wheedle intensively and there's not too much going on they may allow the suspect out of the cell to receive a supervised call on the payphone. Antigona was then still tongue-tied on the phone when she was frightened, so the wheedling fell to me. Me with my BBC accent, my nice teacher's voice and my best, empathetic, deferential mannerisms – 'so kind of you, I know you have so much to do'. It took me at least forty minutes every evening – going through the switchboard, asking for the officer on duty, getting their name, calling them back – 'Hello, PC Angel, we spoke earlier?'

'Isn't that taking rather a lot of Your Time?' asked my husband after a week or so.

'Yup. I expect I'm overinvolved, as usual.'

But, I didn't say, I was strangely enjoying it. I liked winning this game, reporting to Antigona each evening that she had another short phonecall to her cousin sorted out. I liked the sense of so powerfully obliging someone, tying them close to me with gratitude. And I was simply fascinated. It was like when a hole is opened in the road, and all our pipes and wires and the layers of mud and flint we walk over are suddenly exposed, that sewer smell. I didn't know that this could happen; I didn't know it was there.

Hasan, meanwhile, Antigona reported, went rapidly downhill. He wouldn't eat. He couldn't sleep. He smoked and cried all the time. If he were being questioned by the Serbs again he would have spilled the beans a hundred times over and indicted everyone he'd ever met, but fortunately no one ever asked him anything and his solicitor told him to keep schtum. His solicitor was optimistic about the second appeal. Then I called one evening and was told that Hasan had been moved to Dover.

I was writing a radio play about nineteenth-century Tasmania at the time, and my desk was covered with images of prison ships. In my mind, Hasan was in a hulk, shackled to a three-legged stool. I couldn't get through to anyone in Dover, however many numbers I called, however hard I wheedled. Hasan, it seemed, had no rights at all, but sometimes visitors were allowed on a Saturday if they presented themselves in person with their own documents and were happy to be searched.

So I found out about buses to Dover and Antigona bought a carton of cigarettes and the whole family got on the coach for a first glimpse of England's coast. They returned distraught – Antigona had been unable to see Hasan, unable to get inside even the first gate of the hulk – sorry, detention facility. And after that, nothing for weeks. I was relieved of my phone calls, and was glad, as the thrill had long since faded. Antigona seemed to forget about Hasan. This was my first glimpse of this capacity of hers: her ability to withdraw into apparent callousness when a situation is apparently impossible, and to concentrate only on herself and her children. It is the trait, I think, even more than her ingenuity or tenacity, of a real survivor.

Then, as suddenly and as apparently arbitrarily as he had been detained, Hasan's appeal was heard and he got four years' Leave to Remain. Antigona was very happy. Hasan returned to the house in Clissold Park and reclaimed the settee. I found another odd-job task for him and he made another arse of it, standing in my garden for an hour leaning on his rake with his mouth open. 'Letting the wind blow in,' my Grandad would have said, and it was easy to imagine the wind howling around Hasan, scouring the hollow there seemed to be inside him.

The Hasan episode did more than bring me closer to Antigona, though: it also woke me up to some of the complexities of being a Kosovan refugee; it made me ask harder questions of Antigona and of myself; and it sent me to the library to look up some facts. I found out some unexpected things. Such as, although Antigona has learned the power of the name 'Kosovo' here, and though she certainly spent the first thirty-five years of her life entirely in the province as marked on the map, she wouldn't voluntarily call herself Kosovan. She wouldn't say she was Albanian, either, except in a wide, linguistic sense. If it had any meaning here, Antigona would say she comes from the 'Malësi'.

'Malësi' means 'mountains' or 'highlands'. The 'Malësi' is the huge complex of mountains which straddles Albania, Kosovo, Macedonia and Montenegro. It is not marked on the political map, but its people are surely one of the most distinctive in Europe. They have, at least according to themselves, been eking out a living from the mountains' granite slopes and steep valleys forever, or at any rate as far back as the ancient

Greeks. They speak mostly Gheg, a form of Albanian, which is a unique and ancient language. They have been conquered by Romans, Ottomans and Austrians, but never fully accepted any foreign ruler. Their clannish way of life and oral code of law have remained stronger for them than Catholicism, Islam or Communism, and accounts of their epic bolshiness go back two thousand years. To say to an Albanian or a Serb city-dweller that you are a 'Malësor', a mountain man, is like telling one of the good citizens of Edinburgh in 1745 that you are a Highlander. It means 'wild man', 'speaker of incomprehensible antiquated dialect', 'partisan', 'primitive', and 'unreconstructed bronze-age nutcase'. And to say, as Antigona does, that you are a 'mountain woman' is to announce yourself as part woman, part pit-pony: a dauntless, defiant creature of legendary strength and loyalty, capable of anything except city life.

Antigona does indeed love to stress her physical toughness and independence – the mopping, for instance. And she is pleased when I look up the Malësi in the library and come back with questions about her life there – most of the stories, she says, are simply true. Stone Age tattoos, sworn virgins, shaved heads, ritual marriage ceremonies, blood feuds – these are all within her immediate experience. But she tends to assign the more extreme behaviour to people who lived higher up the mountain than herself, or, if something is truly outlandish – rain-dances performed by young girls clad in cabbage leaves – to Herzegovina. 'I was always more city girl,' she says. 'In my head.'

But she has to admit that, at least after her marriage, she was pretty high up the Highlands herself: she lived in a hamlet in the area of Kosovo called Drenica, which is near the small city of Mitrovica. Mitrovica you may have seen on newscasts: a tatty red-roofed town with its small Serb population divided from the majority Albanian one by a famous and bloodily contested bridge. Drenica is high above it, distant green valleys and granite slopes soaring above the cloud-line: a place apparently serene, forgotten by history. Very antique, says Antigona. Very strong heads. High as stink, actually, Drenica.

Drenice, I should say – 'Drenica', with its hard 'c', is the Serb spelling. Antigona says, 'Dren–eesh-a, like Sssh!' For Drenice is also almost entirely Albanian-speaking. Antigona, unlike many Kosovars, knew no Serbs personally: there were none in her village. Nevertheless, Drenice, on the map, is part of Kosovo, not the 'Malësi', and Kosovo is part of Serbia. The Serbs, as much as the Gheg speakers, would say they have 'always been' in Kosovo. The medieval Serbian Golden Age, the time when the Serbs were as prosperous and learned as any people in Europe, the era when they founded their Orthodox Church, was centred in Kosovo. Exquisite ancient churches and monasteries remain to attest this, surrounded now by ramparts of barbed wire. It was in Kosovo in 1389 that the Serbs lost the battle to the Ottomans which signalled the end of their independence and became the subject of their national epic: like Bannockburn, but with a fantastic poem attached. Through centuries of Ottoman rule

Serbs cherished the image of Kosovo, and continued to live there, though in diminishing numbers. Which is why, after the Second World War – when the Serbs, we should perhaps remember, had fought at great cost on our side against Hitler and Albanian and Bulgarian fascists – though the Serb population had shrunk to a 40 per cent minority, it seemed essential to make the province part of Tito's new Yugoslavia.

Antigona thinks well enough of Tito. In her memory, he let them learn Albanian in school and stopped the police being vicious. She is remembering 1974, when Tito, faced with strong stirrings of rebellion, pragmatically relaxed a few rules. What she is not allowing for are the systems Tito set in place, which circumscribed her whole life. During the Tito years, Kosovar Albanians were severely limited in their educational opportunities, were stopped from working in the civil service or the few state-owned industrial enterprises, and were restricted in their movements to other parts of Yugoslavia or even to the Kosovan capital, Pristina. So, even though Antigona's paternal grandparents were educated people, a doctor and former teacher, they were no longer practising their professions by the time she was born, and their children, at least two of whom had made lengthy, strenuous, heartbreaking attempts to finish university, were labouring, like everyone else, on a collective farm. Antigona's mother came from peasant stock and was a superb manager, but she saw no profit from her skill: no one did. So, like everyone else, she got on with having children: Kosovar Albanians, in the sixty years following the war, had the highest birth rate in Europe. Antigona had seven siblings and, we once calculated, 132 first cousins in her generation alone. None of them received more than the most basic education, or it would not be me who would be writing this book.

So Drenice was not serene. After the war, it, and places like it, such as the valley where Antigona was born, steadily filled up with people forbidden to do anything but scratch a basic living from the land or from quarries. These places became crowded with hundreds of lost opportunities, with thousands of blighted lives and nagging grievances; and this among a people with a tradition of blood vengeance. Much of the discontent took a nationalist, pro-Albanian form. A generation of Kosovars dreamed of a better life in a united Albania, a dream which seemed a little less golden in the 1990s, after the passing of the Hoxha regime revealed what contemporary Albania actually looked like. In the meantime, any local Serbs were convenient scapegoats, especially as they still dominated civil service jobs, such as the post office and the police.

As the years passed, though, there were far fewer Serbs: the Kosovar Serbs, like the Russians or Latvians, had a low post-war birth rate, a high abortion rate, and were free besides to move to the more prosperous parts of Yugoslavia. By the time Yugoslavia collapsed, the Serbs were a ten per cent minority in Kosovo, but this did not stop Milosevic seeing the province as a crucial part of his Greater Serbia. As soon as he came to power in 1989, he reimposed Serbo-Croat as the sole official language. Hundreds of Albanian-Kosovar teachers, doctors, and civil servants lost their jobs then, and very many of them went abroad, effectively denuding Kosovo of its tiny Albanian middle class. Places like Drenice were left even more to themselves: its people saw even fewer ways out.

And it was this, the wall round her life, that troubled Antigona, far more than the nationalist issues. Her brothers were involved in the Albanian nationalist movement, she says – so involved they actually had to leave Kosovo in '97, on the boat over to Puglia in Italy – and Fazli was, too, except that he was so incompetent that no one with a brain wanted anything to do with him; but not her. She thought of it as men's stuff, it seems, like Rugby League or poaching: a piece of violent foolishness indulged in to keep their minds away from the many tasks in hand. Despite her horrible sufferings in the war, she is strikingly lacking in prejudice against Serbs. 'It will take a long time to make peace – they will never make peace,' she says of contemporary Kosovo, but when we watch a newscast showing a Serb woman suffering in one of the post-war refugee camps, she simply weeps, and says the woman is like her sister. When I read her Asne Seierstad's *With Their Backs to the World*, she is so overcome by the awfulness of contemporary Serb lives that she begs me to stop. Nor does she ever voice anything but utter scorn for the state of Albania, its leaders, and its corruption.

'Did you ever think that if you were part of Albania things would be better?' I ask, and she shakes her head.

'No really. I wanted to come here.'

'To London?'

'No London. I didn't know about London specially. I wanted to get out. England, Italy, out. No Albania. Out. I saw it on the TV.'

Antigona was eleven when she first saw TV. One of her uncles, the local king of corruption, brought home her village's first set. Her uncle was a difficult man, prone to violent rages, but he always had the volume up, so Antigona would watch through the window, perched in a nearby tree. The generator frequently cut out, and Antigona had no idea, she admits with deep embarrassment, as to what was documentary, newscast, or drama: she took *The Young and the Reckless*, badly dubbed into Italian, to be a fly-on-the-wall documentary of Western European life. She wanted the life she saw on the screen. Not just the new clothes, the shining interiors, the preposterous jewellery, but the freedom. There were women all over the TV doing jobs and making choices. She wanted to join them. She wanted to be in *The Bold and the Beautiful*, because she knew she was; because she wanted some choice, some agency in her own life; because it seemed to her she deserved it.

Sam was watching *Bagpuss* when I asked Antigona about the Dayton Accord of 1995 – I remember the Mice singing 'We Will Fix It' as I mentioned Clinton. So Sam must have been three, and I must have known Antigona nearly two years. The blanks in our conversations, the many things I could not understand, had finally taken me to that question. I am ashamed it took me so long.

I'm also ashamed that I simply assumed the Dayton Accord was a Good Thing. It ended the Bosnian conflict, after all. I remembered Clinton looking triumphant and Madeleine Albright being fabulous and lots of footage of that bridge in Sarajevo and feeling relieved that the shootings would stop. But, says Antigona, as the Mice sing 'we will mend it', Dayton was when her brothers joined something like the Kosovan Liberation Army, a step which led very rapidly to their arrest, torture, and flight from the country. 'Before that,' says Antigona, 'they were for Rugova.'

Back to the library for more rapid Googling. Ibrahim Rugova, the first President of Kosovo, whom Antigona still regards as a hero, was one of the university teachers expelled by Milosevic. He went to Paris, and organized a 'government in exile' from there, asking Albanians earning abroad for 'taxes' and instigating a campaign of peaceful resistance and non-cooperation with Serb edicts within Kosovo. Rugova hoped that his peaceful tactics would capture the sympathies of the international community while it was focused on Yugoslavia and waking up to the outrages of Bosnia and the true nature of Milosevic. His movement had a lot of support within and outside Kosovo, and all its hopes were centred on Dayton. Surely, they thought, the world would not throw Kosovo to Milosevic, knowing what they knew. Surely the reports of atrocities already coming out of Kosovo would mean the province was in some way protected, that the Kosovars would get some level of self-determination?

But they didn't, and we didn't. We did not fix it, did not mend it. Dayton did nothing for the Kosovars: the province was given to Milosevic to exert his waning powers upon. And so, inevitably, Rugova's campaign lost credibility in Kosovo, and men like Antigona's brothers were not alone in turning to more violent groups and attacking Serb targets such as post offices and police stations. Some of the attacks were crude and savage, and Milosevic's pariah state responded even more savagely: this is when the stories of atrocities start, in '96, '97; not in '99, when the world woke up to them.

'Antigona,' I ask, 'what happened to your brothers?' and she turns red, opens and shuts her lips, and I don't press her.

One day, Antigona is very late. I was going to leave Sam with her and I miss an appointment and am very cross. Then she comes in, ashen-faced, and sits down. There was a fire in her street – a kitchen fire. A woman came running out, waving a burning tea towel. Smoke, there was lots of smoke. The firemen came, the children had gone to school already, it was all OK. She wanted to help but she forgot all her English. She wanted to help but she didn't know what to do. She wanted to help but the firemen came, the children had gone to school already, it was all OK. She was sorry she was late but she couldn't get past there. She sat on the wall and couldn't get past there. There was a fire, and a woman running. There was smoke and she sat on the wall and was not able to get off until a fireman told her to and then she stumbled along to my house.

I ask again, and again in a different way, but Antigona still won't tell me what happened to her brothers. I suspect something dire, something of a piece with the probable fate of her parents and three married sisters. Because they are missing and she can find no trace about them. The church people have been to the Red Cross with Antigona, several times; they have peered at the lists from Macedonian refugee camps – she is positive they would have gone to Macedonia – and found no record. The area where her birth family lived was a significant one. Everyone there had a 'bad war'. Yet Antigona always talks of her family in the present tense. She says that her mother is a strong person and her family will be living somewhere where there were not good records, records aren't everything. When she gets enough money together, she will go and look for them. It is too many people to disappear, she says. I have no idea if this could be true or not. I have no idea how she copes.

My own mother gets ill around this time, with a condition which turns out to be treatable but at first appears to be galloping leukaemia. She comes to visit me when they are doing the tests, insists on coming to the playground, and collapses, suddenly as a tall pine falling, at the bottom of the slide. The thought of her death is an end point in my mind, a door through which I cannot imagine walking. No one very close to me has died. I know Antigona has walked through that door and kept going, and I am learning from her some of what that means, of the many tricks the mind plays to allow you to cope, and the revenges it takes, later.

I keep asking about the war, though. More facts leak on me: why Antigona expected me to know what 'Drenice' meant, for instance; why she flushes when she says it. It's like saying you're from the West Bank or the Falls Road: it was the very crucible of the Kosovan conflict. It was where the famous Donje Prekaze incident occurred, for instance, when fifty members of one Albanian family were killed in a Serb attack on the Jeshari family compound; it was also where the massacre of the Delijaj family occurred, when Human Rights Watch actually managed to witness and record the deaths of twenty-one people, all of them civilians, at the hands of Serb police. Five of those victims were children, one a toddler with a dummy round his neck. They shot a nine-month-pregnant woman dead; they left the corpse of a nursing mother on top of her living six-week-old baby. And Drenice got the UK into the war: it was another massacre there in March '99 and mass demonstrations at the subsequent funerals in Mitrovice which finally led to the involvement of NATO.

I'm also learning: despite this, the war wasn't exactly what I thought it was. It wasn't Bosnia. Half a million Bosniaks died in the conflict in their country; 6,000 men were killed in a day at Srebrenica. At the height of the Kosovan war, Jamie Shea, William Cohen, Robin Cook and Geoff Hoon made claims of a similar genocide in Kosovo: of 100,000 Albanian deaths, of mass graves containing thousands of bodies, and I believed them, because of Bosnia. I didn't notice, in the years following the war, that those figures were being revised, slowly and steadily, downwards. The toll in Kosovo is now estimated at 7,000–10,000, including 2,000 bodies found in mass graves. At least 2,000 more Kosovars are still missing.

Which is not to say that I am taking the war more lightly. Flora's injury, I am learning, is not just in her hip; is not just the fault lines visible on the X-ray. The Kosovan war dealt in fear and shame and long-term suffering: it almost specialized in it. The war had a pattern. First, the KLA would attack a Serb target – policemen or paramilitaries, but Serb or even Albanian postmen and schoolteachers and park rangers, too. In return, and in fear, the Serbs redoubled the terror. The Delijaj family, for example, was massacred in reprisal for the deaths of seven Serb policemen. That same week, in the same reprisal operation, the nearby small town of Golubovac was shelled. The population fled and the town was looted and burned. Then Serb police rounded up several thousand refugees. Fourteen men were finally selected, interrogated, abused and executed: a relatively small death toll. Thousands, though, were left devastated, homeless and terrified, and they went out and spread the fear in wider rings yet: as far as Antigona's village, for instance. 'Internal displacement', said Human Rights Watch at the time, was one of the most devastating effects of the war. 'Internal displacement' meant losing your home, your assets, being a beggar, being terrified, being ashamed. In Drenice alone more than 200 villages were destroyed and at least 300,000 people were 'internally displaced'. The time Antigona spent among them, with a three-year-old and an injured daughter, is one she still does not talk about.

Also, I always thought wars stopped, had an end point. This one didn't, though, any more than it started on a single day. It lives on in Antigona's mind and body, and it lives on in Kosovo. Immediately after the war, 170,000 Serbian refugees streamed across the Kosovan border with tales which echoed those of the Albanians: the burning and looting of villages, being hunted through the hills by their former neighbours. Very many of them are still in refugee camps in Serbia now, chewing over their wrongs, wondering who is living in their houses; they have not been given Exceptional Leave to Remain in the UK, nor airlifts. No leading politician has paused to look into their tear-stained faces for the truth, though I am sure, and so is Antigona, that they have several truths to tell. And we certainly haven't paused to look into the faces of the 20,000 Roma, Turks, and even Bosniaks who followed the Serbs, any more than Antigona's city gent would have paid for her taxi if he'd thought she was a Gypsy.

Ibrahim Rugova did at last become President of Kosovo, only to fall foul of the Albanians' national vice, smoking, and die of lung cancer. Antigona wept for him. He has proved impossible to replace. Kosovo, as I write, is still an anomalous, unresolved state.

And yet: however terrible the war, however much Antigona suffered, she never says that she regrets the house she was forced from or the people she left behind. Her life there was shattered, but the shattering set her free.

Time passes. I have known Antigona for three years. Sam is nearly four and suddenly able to go swimming in the big pool with Ylli, whom he worships. I take both boys regularly, most Sundays. I have suspended my enquiries into Antigona's story for the moment, because I don't seem to be able to get past certain points. It's not just her brothers. The more I find out about the war, the more certain dates and times become fixtures in my mind, the more some things just don't stack up. It's the dates. The months. March '99 Antigona and her family were expelled from their homes. December they arrived here. Had they been in the woods for nine months? In the cousin's house? I ask about it, at different times and in different ways, but each time Antigona's English mysteriously deserts her. Each time she turns away.

Then, one Sunday, on the way out from the pool, we meet a slight dark man who is evidently embarrassed to see Ylli. Ylli nevertheless rushes up and has a long conversation in Albanian.

'That's my uncle,' he tells me, on the way to the bus.

'Ah,' I say, 'your mother's cousin. She told me.'

'No,' says Ylli. 'My uncle. Mum's brother. Her *brother*.'

'Your mum hasn't got any brothers – they disappeared in the war.'

'She's got three brothers. That's the middle one.'

So I ask Antigona, and she tells me Ylli is foolish. That is cousin Djon, as she'd told me. Yes, a distant cousin. The one with the motorbike. After that, she doesn't speak to me for a week.

Then she announces she has to tell me something. We are tidying Sam's room, and for once she empties her hands, and sits on the bed. 'This is the true,' she says. 'I want to tell you the true.'

'You don't have to,' I say, alarmed.

'I want to. You are my sister here. I want to tell the true.'

And this is what she tells me. It is about how she got here, and what is true.

She was living in Drenice, all true. (Drenice, Drenice, the living baby under her mother's corpse, her mouth full of her mother's blood, the old man burnt upright in his armchair, the young men kneeling by the roadside to be killed and buried like cattle, all true. Look up those reports some time, Google the name in an idle moment: you will retch, you will weep, your hair will stand on end.)

The Serbs came to her house, all true. Flora and the roof, all true. The burning of the village and flight into the forest, the dog – Antigona was never that bothered about the dog. Dogs have fleas. But Fazli had already been away for months, not days, and they did know where he was. He had run away early in '98 after a not-exactly KLA outrage, more like a failed robbery, but with KLA guys involved. He was living near Naples, he had some sort of job, and he had called to a neighbour's mobile phone. Antigona had a number for him.

The cousin's house, that was right, but it was on the Albanian, not the Kosovan side of the border, and she didn't stay there long. They had no money, the cousin was desperate to get rid of her, Fazli sent nothing, the NATO bombs had not yet started to fall and there was no end to the war in sight. So Antigona decided to go to Naples and find Fazli. She went the only the way she knew of, in a boat, by night, over the straits to Puglia.

Antigona can hardly tell this part. She sits on my son's bed and weeps. She took the family. Ylli was only three, Flora could still hardly walk. It was night. There were hundreds of people on the beach, but not many women and no other children. The boats were small – rubber dinghies with outboard motors, the sort we use for lifeboats. The smugglers started loading people onto the boats; so many that they sank lower and lower in the water.

Their turn. They hung their shoes round their necks and waded into the sea, which was cold; it was only May. Mihane scrambled over the slippery, inflated-rubber side. She hauled Flora after her. Antigona hung on to the side with one hand and lifted Ylli up for the girls to pull aboard, but the engines revved and the boat surged forward and she and the baby were flung into the dark sea. Ylli surfaced; then sank.

Antigona had been a tomboy; she had learned to swim in the river. With all her tomboy knowledge and all her grown-woman strength and all her mother's longing for her child she swam after Ylli and dived down in the place he had gone beneath the waves and grabbed his little round limbs and swam after the boat and flung him aboard. The boat was gaining speed, the engines revving, the propellers turning that could suck Antigona under and chop her to pieces, as had happened to many already and as happened to another woman on that beach that night, but as did not now happen to Antigona who instead grasped the rubber edge of the dinghy, swollen and cold as a drowned limb, and flung herself over the side and found all her children there alive.

But that was only the beginning. Then there was the journey over the dark sea, the overloaded boat nearly upright in the water, a brisk wind, salt water drying on freezing limbs, Ylli traumatized and stiff on his mother's knee, calling out for the moon. Then being abandoned at dawn on the bone-bare Puglia beach and climbing a cliff and walking three hours over stones. Mihane had no shoes and Flora had her injured hip, and Ylli was only three. There was nothing to drink. They were terribly afraid of the Carabinieri. Then there was the getting into the town and the begging, yes, begging – Antigona can hardly bear to recount it – of bread for the children and change for a phone box, and then the calling of Fazli, who had no help for them, and the getting on a train, and the hiding in the corridors and the toilet because they had no tickets, and getting out at the station Fazli had said, and at least he was there, but he had nowhere for them and they slept that night in a stable so perhaps this was a Christmas story after all.

Except it wasn't a wood stable with snug straw and warm-breathed animals – more of an empty barn with barred windows and a sloping concrete floor. And this wasn't the Railway Children either, with a lovely long-lost Daddy coming back; this was Fazli, who was stupid and feckless only on his very best days.

So the family was thrown back on its own resources. Antigona got a job. A cleaning job with a posh family who sat her on a separate table at meals and served her plain pasta while they ate meat. She hadn't much Italian yet but she understood them perfectly. Flora got a job, too, serving in a shop, and Mihane minded Ylli.

But they are attractive people to help, Antigona and her beautiful doe-eyed daughters, her gorgeous smiling son, and even in a godforsaken poverty-stricken suburb of Naples, a place without made-up roads or reliable sanitation, they found themselves cared for. Neighbours brought them meals, first plate and second plate, says Antigona, who had never had such a luxury in her life. Antigona picked up Italian very quickly; she knew it really, from the telly, and soon made friends. There was one woman in particular, Giuseppina, who ran a small bar. Ylli, too, learned Italian and crowed out 'Ciao, ciao' in his throaty voice to the boys on their scooters, and soon found himself taken out for rides, a local mascot. Antigona left the job with the plain pasta people and got a better one with a nice family who had a shoe shop. She found a new home, a room with no electricity and a single tap.

So that would have been fine, or better than nothing, except for Fazli. Fazli had always been drunk, had never worked much, and had always beaten Antigona up, but here in Italy his problems were much worse. He got day-labouring jobs, but instantly bet away his earnings. He did the same with Antigona's when he could get hold of them. He went to the shop where Flora worked and took her first week's wages from the proprietor and spent them. He beat up the girls, now, as well as Antigona. One day, when Antigona was fighting him back, he took Ylli and disappeared with him. She went to the police but they laughed in her face and asked for her identity card. No one would help her, here. Fazli didn't bring Ylli back till nightfall and then he raped her and beat her again.

Months passed, and Antigona became convinced that Fazli was planning to sell Flora into prostitution. When she tells me this I at first dismiss it: it smacks of Evelyn Waugh, white traders, absurdity. But it is not absurd, at all. Very many of Europe's prostitutes are young Albanian girls, very many of them are launched from Italy, and someone must be selling them, so why not a semi-employed gambling-addicted drunken Albanian running with criminal company rather too clever for him, even if he is the girl's father? Flora was nearly fourteen with wavy hair to her thighs. She would raise a good price.

So Antigona started hiding money with Pina at the bar, and did something else too. She went through

Fazli's jacket and got the number, then used the public phone and called her brothers.

'Your brothers?'

'Yes. Clissold Park. Agim. Driton – who Ylli saw. Hasan. My brothers.'

Her brother. Her brothers. The Clissold Park people are her brothers: Agim, Driton and Hasan. I am scarlet at my own credulity. Of course, of course: a brother, who takes you in at Christmas, a brother, whom you call every night when he is in prison. My mind is so full of the clunking together of the blatantly obvious, the shifting of furniture, I can hardly hear Antigona. But she is pressing on with her story. This is very different from the first time she told me what had happened to her. That had the quality of theatre: this is something uncorked.

You see, someone in Naples – part of the Albanian underworld that Fazli is so ambitious to join – had met Agim, the eldest brother, in England. He gave Fazli Agim's mobile phone number, and Fazli called him. The three brothers were still together, they were working in a mirror factory in London, they had some sort of papers, they had a home.

Antigona had hopes of her big brother. When she was fifteen and he was twenty she would wash his white shirt for him every night and iron it fresh for the morning. If it was his trousers as well, she would stay up all night over the task, because you couldn't get to the stove to boil the water before midnight. Also, when she'd been married a few years, she'd told Agim about Fazli, and he did the proper thing: viz., came round with a Kalashnikov and threatened to shoot him. Driton, too – her handsome brother, the one she called her twin. He would not desert her.

So Antigona calls the number. Agim is happy to hear from her. He is a big man in England now, and will help his family get there. They need to go to Brussels where he has a connection – but why is Antigona calling, not Fazli? Antigona explains. Agim freezes at once. Antigona must stay with her husband, he says, for the family honour. He has no help to offer her unless she comes with her husband.

So Antigona confides in Pina, who agrees to help her. One morning, as soon as Fazli has left the house, Pina borrows her brother's car and drives Antigona and the children to the station. They get on a train north. Antigona has taken Fazli's phone. When they arrive in Rome, Pina calls her on it. She is in a police station. Fazli is trying to get her arrested for abducting his children, trafficking his daughter, and stealing his mobile. Pina is terrified. She begs them to come back and show themselves. Flora, overwhelmed with guilt, backs her up, but Antigona knows a trap when she sees its jaws. She tells Pina what is exactly the case: the police have no evidence and Fazli has no papers and no money and is very tiresome, and therefore the police will throw him out and Pina will soon be released. Antigona will move on.

They get on another train to Paris. The girls don't have tickets, none of them have passports, they hide in the toilets when the inspectors come, and a miracle happens at the French border, when the passport official looks them up and down and then nods them through. Antigona's special charm, perhaps, or maybe it is the thought of Christmas coming and the sight of a woman and a baby so evidently fleeing from Herod.

As they rattle under the Alps, they make friends with an elderly professor. At the Gare du Nord, he finds them a cafe where they can sit till dawn with the sandwiches he buys them, and when six o'clock comes the cafe owner gives them milk. Then they get on the train to Brussels. That is where Fazli said the lorries to England went from. The station there is larger and more threatening than the Gare du Nord. They have been awake for two days. They have no money – not even enough for the toilet. Their phone has stopped working. They walk around. They look at the Eurostar with its heavily guarded platform. Outside, they find a garage with many lorries and Albanian men hanging around, but Antigona's nerve fails her. She doesn't know what to do; she doesn't know where to start. She begs money for a phone box and calls her brother. 'Where is your husband?' he says. And when Antigona explains, he puts the phone down.

Despair. The red-faced panic, the spluttering tears, the walking in circles, the awful sweats. What to do with it? Where to put it? Antigona looked at the children she had carried from the burning village, snatched from the sea, hauled half across a continent, and didn't know how to contain herself. She blurted out the whole story to the girls, how Uncle Agim wasn't going to help them after all, and after a while Flora went off and begged some money and called him herself.

After that, we return the original story. Except that Agim organized the lorry, and they weren't in it for more than a day, and they did know they should be heading for London. Ylli and the thumbed lift, the Good Person of Gravesend, the city gent and the twenty-quid taxi: all true, true – except that Flora had been given the church address by Agim along with clear instructions on what not to say to Immigration, and she held on to it all the way. Christmas morning and the bells of London – all true, truer than ever.

But this is what happens next. Agim, Driton and Hasan came round. They took Antigona to PhoneShop International on the Hackney Road, and stood round her in the sweaty little plywood booth: Agim, who had been so slender in the days when she handed him a thin white shirt hot from the iron each morning, was now a squat, plump man, his belly resting on his hairy hands. Driton, just a year younger than her, the wiry, shy boy she had fought and played with her whole childhood, was distant, embarrassed, his lovely dark eyes avoiding hers. And Hasan, baby Hasan, whom she barely knew as he was still toddling when she was married off, was a man, a worried, bearded man in a suit.

Agim was spokesman. They offered her a deal. Either she could, via a fax to Pina's bar, contact Fazli, apologize, and offer him, brokered by the brothers, a lorry to join them, then pay the brothers back for both passages (£13,000). Or she could never see any of her family again except while paying them back for her own passage (£10,000). After some thought, Antigona sent the fax to Fazli, giving him the good news.

'Because of Shame?' I say. I can't bear this ending. I want to weep.

'Yeah, ' says Antigona.

'Well, I think – they should be ashamed.' And she nods and I see that one of the reasons she told the story was so that I would say that. So that I, who have become one of her gauges of Englishness, of how things are here, in the New World, would listen to her story and say that.

Things are at once easier between Antigona and me, now that the deceit is out of the way. We talk a lot more, retelling stories without the embarrassing lies. I understand, now, the hold that Agim has on her, the balm of Driton's kindness, her anxiety for Hasan. It all makes sense. One thing we do not discuss is why she maintained the deceit in the first place. We don't need to – I understood at once. She didn't tell me her story when we met because she didn't know me, and the information is dangerous for me to have, because it could affect her asylum claim.

The problem, in asylum terms, is this: in Antigona's first escape story, when she comes directly here from Drenice, she is a refugee pure and simple, someone fleeing her own country because she is in 'reasonable fear', as the legal definition has it, of her life. But in this new version, the case is not so clear. She could, an interviewing officer might point out, have stopped in Albania and received asylum; she could have asked for asylum in Italy, which is an EU country; she could have returned to Kosovo in the summer of 1999; she could even have asked for asylum in Belgium. In all these places, legally speaking, she could have received protection.

It is easy to prove that Flora was maimed by Serb policemen: it shows up in the X-ray. It is harder to argue, and difficult to believe, too, when you have grown up in a civil state, that Antigona did not know she could have claimed asylum in Italy or Albania. She didn't know she could have asked for help there from anyone. She had no experience of neutral lawgivers. She had not heard of police who protect women. She had not heard of Human Rights, any more than she had heard of the Channel Tunnel. When she had asked the Italian police for help to get Ylli from her husband, they had laughed at her. She genuinely did not know and could not imagine that in Italy or Belgium or even Albania it is not legal for husbands to kill their wives. She thought Fazli was going to kill her and sell her daughter, and the only protection she knew of, under her code, was her brothers, so that is where she went. On paper, though, Antigona left a job in Italy and came here to join prosperous relatives. That could be enough to make her into what Mark and the *Daily Mail* and even this Labour government call an economic migrant, not a refugee.

And it is true that when Antigona left Albania she was not just running from a war; true that when she got into the lifeboat, when she fled across Europe, she also had *The Bold and the Beautiful* in her mind. She did hope that, apart from staying alive, she might raise herself and her children above desperate poverty. She thought, even, that she herself might live somewhere where she would not be regularly raped and beaten with the sanction of an entire community. It was her hopes, these bold, tremendous hopes, which carried her along her terrible journey, and a few years down the line, it is these same hopes that will do her in.

FREEDOM

Antigona and I are out on the Marshes. I'm with Sam; she's minding one of her other employers' children. We quite often find ourselves like this – one of the things we have in common is that we like to be Out, Out, with our children, whatever the weather. A police helicopter is buzzing over us, circling, returning. They do this a lot round our way, whizzing about with heat-seeking cameras and such, thrilling the little ones and making me fume about squandered resources.

Antigona dumps her pushchair with me. 'I'm going to play,' she says. She pulls her coat over her head and dashes from our group of bushes to the shelter of a nearby wall, then across to another, where she squats down. Sure enough, the helicopter turns and swoops round, comes close enough to beat the air and make it shake. I am horrifyingly embarrassed. *Mortified*: my legs feel like lead. I can't hear my own voice.

'Antigona! What the hell are you doing?'

She makes another dash, coat over head, and disappears. The helicopter is so close I can see the pilot. The noise is frightful. I wave, frantically, point at the pushchair, the little children who, judging by their open mouths, are screaming against the deafening roar. Suddenly, Antigona pops out of the bush behind me and grabs her pushchair. She shakes her hair to her shoulders; she is the picture of a nanny. She waves merrily to the helicopter and it buzzes off. The quiet is overwhelming.

'Why are you so scared, Kate? They can't do anything to you! In this country, no one is allowed to kill you!'

3

Dirty, Clean, and the Kanun of Lek

In a certain sense, this was why I felt so close to the others in the Greek class. They, too, knew this beautiful and harrowing landscape; they had had the same experience of looking up from their books with fifth-century eyes and finding the world disconcertingly sluggish and alien, as if it were not their home.

Donna Tartt, *The Secret History*

The importance of the Kanun to the ordinary life of the Albanians of Kosovo and the Malësi can hardly be exaggerated.

Noel Malcolm, *Kosovo: A Short History*

Things Antigona Knows How to Do and I Don't: No. 2

WASH AND LAY OUT BRIDAL SHEETS

Bridal sheets should be new, but you know that new is not clean enough. So:

You rub them with home-made lye soap until they are slimy as a piece of liver.

You scrub them against a washboard until the sweat springs from your forehead.

Or bash them with a pestle in a wooden churn.
And/or boil them in a large cauldron over wood you have gathered for this purpose.
And wring them out with another woman and twist them into a heavy wet coil.
You carry them, with the other women, to the river, and rinse them in the full current until no more clouds or tendrils of soap will issue from them.
With another woman, pulling and tugging, you peg them out in the tenterground in full sun, so they can bleach. They will be critiqued by the other women at this point, and if there is, for example, a grass stain, you will start again at the first step.
In a shuffling, flag-waving dance with the other women, you fold them: they are voluminous now, light, and sweet smelling. You carry them home.
You iron them with little flat irons heated on the stove or with larger irons filled with hot embers until they are warm and smooth as the inside of a baby's arm.
You lay them on the bed, ceremoniously, with the other women. Put the special half-sheet on last, carefully, laughing, in the place where the hips will rest.
On the evening of the wedding, when the half-sheet is thrown out of the bedroom, you will read, with the other women, the sentence of the stain.

Things I Know How to Do and Antigona Doesn't: No. 2

WORK MY WASHING MACHINE

But it doesn't take very long to explain.

It is one of the first things Antigona asks me when she comes to my house. I have not asked her to do laundry, but she does it anyway, and when she is distressed she will wash anything: cushion covers, floor cloths, rugs, often together, disastrously, on 'Hot'. We may find the sight of women folding sheets lovely, or admire a field of thorns blossoming with laundry, but Antigona is with Marcel Duchamp: the washing machine is much more beautiful. Each bundle thrust in, each shuddering spin, is a load which she does not have to boil, or pound, or scrub, or haul, or peg. She was used to that work, born to that work, but she hated it, every bit of it, every time, just as much as I would, were I to find myself doing it.

In the first months she works for me, Antigona and I have a strong friendly feeling towards each other which we do not quite know what to do with. Her English is still halting: my ignorance of the Malësi is still total. So we stand in the kitchen, smiling, looking for something to gossip about. There is Sam and his blondness, but that runs short. Child conversations always seem to lead to ones I find harder: about how clean she, Antigona, is and has always been, how clean she keeps her children, a wonder to her mother and all her neighbours, and about how clean or otherwise other people's houses are, or even their front steps. These conversations make me anxious, because I think she is commenting on how untidy I am (very). It reminds me of my mother trying to find new ways to tell me to clean my room, and it has the same effect: to make me change the subject – but to what?

Well, there is the cost of things, but here too we are far apart. I have been brought up not to mention money, or to mention it in an encoded way – 'good value', 'quality item', 'solid investment' – which indicates at once unworldliness and prudence. But Antigona mentions money all the time: she grew up in poverty and under communism, so how and where to get cheap goods is crucial information. Telling me the day and the halal butchers where I can buy an entire fresh sheep for less than I generally pay for a joint of organic beef is, for her, a favour, an act of sharing. She also likes to save me vouchers for stores which she thinks I, as an improvident person, might shop in, like Boots. I take the vouchers, but I am sniffy, or at best patronizing, about the tips. I have lived in our area for five years, but there are many shops I have always walked past because the smell of coriander, offal and damp cardboard is too much for me – shops where Antigona is quite at home, sniffing the tomatoes straight from the box, directing the worn-thin butcher's knife on the bloodied chopping board. After a few months, Antigona picks up on my incurable snobberies, and confines her shopping point-scoring habit to picking up my Taste the Difference and Organic Veg packets to scan the prices, while raising her eyebrows so high, she risks injury to her forehead.

But by now, we have found new topics. There is business: letter-writing, Lunar House, our battles with the Council. She tells me about her children, about 'Clissold Park' and Fazli. We establish reference points, nicknames, become able to mutually deplore. Especially Fazli. On this subject I do not patronize, as I am in awe of her resilience and defiance. I respond to his surveillance of her, his phone calls, his menaces, with honest outrage, which she likes and doesn't always get from her Kosovan friends. One day she tells me Fazli has accused her of sleeping with all of her employers because she had been seen going to work wearing a pair of loose summer trousers, which he declared were pyjamas. This in itself would not have been so bad, except that the Clissold Park people had not been supportive. They said the trousers looked like pyjamas, too, and maybe she should quit her jobs.

'They're just obsessed with sex,' I say. 'All of them. Fazli, Clissold Park. They're just dirty-minded.'

Antigona looks at me intently, then smiles, then laughs. It is a new thought, a cheering one. She translates an old formula to fit her feelings.

'They are like country boy,' she says. 'I am more city girl.'

Generally, though, on clothes, we still arrive at an impasse. Antigona always wants me to comment on what she is wearing. It is often new. She favours tight trousers, vest tops, and sequinned T-shirts; she has a great figure and can carry them off, and I say so. But she always looks for more: specifically, how much would I say it cost? And I squirm, because I have already guessed: not much. I would be very comfortable answering the questions, 'Too camp, do you think? Bit OTT bling-bling? Bit muttony? Do you *get* it's ironic?' *Irony*. I can't explain *ironic* clothes to Antigona, and I don't want to, because in the face of someone who owned just two or three outer garments for most of her adult life, *irony* seems rather spoilt and nasty, all of a sudden. Irony suddenly seems like another code for money, for always having had money. So I guess a high price for the T-shirt. So I am astounded at her bargain.

Even then, I know I am still not getting my comments (which she always directs to tightness and shortness) right. She is appealing to a code I don't understand, one which is of a piece with her tedious obsession with virginity: Who is a virgin in Britain, and who isn't. Are all the girls in short skirts really prostitutes? Do all British girls lose their virginity at twelve? What about the mothers who show their tummies – are they prostitutes on the side? What about all the women who come in groups to restaurants, dressed in tight clothes – some of them are married, are they cheating on their husbands? Poor husbands, how can they marry a girl who is not a virgin?

This conversation gets on my nerves. It is not a subject I've ever managed to be interested in, even when I was a teenager. I remember listening in to girls' accounts of doing anything but 'it' – oral sex, elaborate frotting – and asking, beetle-browed, bookish weirdo that I was, 'But what on earth is the moral difference?', to general smirks. It seemed very clear to me, even then, that a man who wanted a virgin wanted power and an imprint of himself, and that a woman who cherished her 'cherry' was playing along with a male agenda. Did we think we were cakes? Why celebrate passivity or ignorance? No one ever offered a reply to my arguments; they just opened their eyes very wide and said that was fine but they thought there was 'something nice' about 'saving themselves', in the same way they thought it was 'nice' when boys opened doors for them – though they did also want a career.

I stopped having this argument sometime in my twenties, because I didn't know any virgins any more. I am thoroughly annoyed to be having it in my late thirties. But now Antigona is looking at my wedding photos, pleased to see me in something fitted, for once (she despises my baggy clothes), and silvery. This demonstrates, she is saying, that I must have been a virgin when I married, wasn't I?

'Certainly not,' I growl.

And watch my kitchen rock her, and then return her to her feet. But my husband was my first boyfriend?

'No.'

She opens her mouth. She closes it. She stores the information, and will return to it and digest it later. And then, without missing a beat, we return to the question of whether Flora and Mihane should be allowed to go to an asylum-seekers' youth group on a Wednesday, or whether such an activity might stain their honour, as there are boys there. This really gets my goat.

'Look,' I say. 'They've got to go to school, right?

Well, if they're going to lose their virginities, they can do it at the bus stop if they want to! You've got to let them go. You've got to trust them. You don't have a choice.'

To my surprise, Antigona nods, pleased. 'That's what I said – to my friend. To Clissold Park. But he say Flora shouldn't go to school. She is too big a girl. Men will look. Anything can happen.'

And I lose my temper. 'He is completely cracked! He is medieval! Look, this is England. Flora and Mihane are growing up in England. Flora needs to go to school to get qualifications and get a job. She needs to do things. She needs to choose who to be! Being a virgin – no one cares here. It's not a career path. And anyway – what the hell has it got to do with Clissold Park?'

This is before I find out about the brothers. Antigona flushes and moves away to the sink. I note that she is offended, but I decide I may as well carry on ranting, for my own peace of mind.

'Being a virgin is a passive state. It's just something you haven't done yet. It can't be the main reason for valuing you as a person. That's vile. It's just about giving men what they want, like, "Look, here you are, here's a nice clean pot for you to plant your seed!" Well, Flora isn't a pot. She's a person. A very clever person. She can do all sorts of things.'

I stop, out of breath. Antigona has turned from the sink and is giving me the full beam of her concentration. She narrows her eyes, nods.

'That's what I think,' she says. 'I agree with you.'

*

It isn't just Fazli who follows her around, I notice. Clissold Park does a lot of it, too, in his taxi, shadowing her, lurking outside my door. I can't work it out. Is it because she is Muslim?

News reports often stressed the differences between Muslim Albanian Kosovars and Serbo-Croat-speaking, Serbian Orthodox Kosovars (the minority of Albanian Kosovar Catholics was rarely mentioned: a distinction too far, perhaps), and Antigona is indeed Albanian and, nominally, Muslim. Her village had been Muslim, she says, for a very long time, since the Turks: most of the Malësi was converted during Ottoman rule. But, even from our very early conversations, she is clearly of little faith.

'The Muslims here, they don't help us,' is one of her first complaints. 'The mosque, you go there, they do nothing. The church, you go there, they do everything for you. Maybe I turn Christian.'

'Really?' But she is mocking me.

'No. To be Christian, you believe Jesus he got up again, yeah? When he is dead?'

'Yes. That's about the size of it.'

'But that one is not true. Who can believe that? Honestly?'

When Ramadan comes around, she is eager to eat lunch with me, to demonstrate that she is breaking the fast. In fact, she asks me to pass the ham.

'Do you keep Ramadan in your village?'

'No really. Some – the old people. No me. I fast anyway – there is not enough to eat.'

And Little Eid? And Eid-ul-Fitr? Celebrations – but

minor ones. The major festivals were secular and traditional: New Year, when sheep were roasted and gifts given, and Spring, when new lamb was eaten among the glorious wild flowers. Pigs were not kept or eaten, but sheep do far better in the mountains anyway, and certainly the men drank alcohol: Antigona is keen to tell me about her mother's home-made raki. Everyone swallowed great snifters of it, often at breakfast.

Shia? Sunni? Wahabi? These are all meaningless terms to Antigona. Did she get married in the mosque? She laughs.

'I've never gone in the mosque.'

'Never?'

'No at all. The men go, sometimes. No me. It is only here the Albanians get Muslim.'

'Because of the mosque?' Our local mosque is of the Saudi-funded, evangelical, Wahabi sort.

'Yeah – that mosque. I met a man on the Hackney Road last week, Albanian man, and he will not shake hands with me!' She mimes the Albanian's limp gestures of disgust, and hoots with laughter. 'Because I am woman! He has grown a beard! He is wearing pyjamas! Can you believe it?'

'But in the Malësi, being Muslim, that is not the important thing?'

'No, tradition is the important thing. Opinion. What people say.'

When we have known each other a year, Antigona tells me about a man. Tony. He is Flora and Mihane's school counsellor, appointed to help them with their refugee status and broken home. He came round to Antigona's house in his official capacity, but now has called her unofficially, asked her for 'one coffee'.

'He shouldn't do that,' I say.

'Because he is black?' she says. I flush, outraged.

'No! Because he is a counsellor. It's against the rules. I didn't know he was black.'

'His Mum and Dad come from Jamaica. He is handsome man, actually.'

'I'm sure. Are you going?'

'One coffee – it is nothing. Like friends.'

'Of course it is. Go.'

She goes. Then he asks her out to dinner. She goes, after a lengthy consultation with me about skirt lengths. The dinner is a great success. I am still suspicious of Tony, because of his job, and because he seems overly interested in hearing her problems, counselling her, but there is no denying he has cheered her up. For a week, he calls her several times a day, and she appears flushed, glossy and flattered. Then, overnight, she is crushed, turns up yellow-faced on my doorstep with her newly bobbed hair sticking in all directions.

Mihane and Flora had twigged what was going on. They had made a huge scene, weeping and hitting and rending garments.

'They felt betrayed by Tony,' I said.

'No! Is me. They do not want me with any man.'

'You've got the right to a life.'

But Antigona is emptied of her usual defiance. No,

she says, no. She has given in to her daughters. She has sworn on Ylli's life never to speak to Tony again, nor go out with any man.

'They're teenagers,' I say. 'They'll get over it.'

'No just my daughters,' says Antigona flatly. 'Everyone think that.'

'Clissold Park?'

'Yeah. Everyone. Tradition. Opinion.'

'Like the Kanun of Lek?' I venture. I've been doing some reading. Antigona perks up. She almost laughs.

'How do you know that?' she says, delighted.

'When I came here,' says Antigona, 'after I was here six months, I see what is the life here. I watch *EastEnders*, I start to understand English, I see the people. And I realize – it is not the law here that men can kill their wives.'

Whereas in the Malësi, the law says that men can kill their wives, and grooms are given a bullet on their wedding day by the bride's family for that purpose. Not Albanian law as recorded in Pristina or Tirana, that is, but the traditional code of the mountains: the system of penalties and customs known as the Kanun of Lek. 'Kanun' comes from the Greek word which gives us 'canon', 'Lek' from A*lek*sander Dukagjin, a legendary fourteenth-century member of the leading Dukagjin (Duke John) family. 'Lek' is said to have laid down the code, though it wasn't actually written till the nineteenth century. The Kanun was the most important set of ideas in Antigona's upbringing: holier than the pronouncements of the Imam, and far, far more significant and immediate than any law written down in Pristina or Belgrade.

The Kanun of Lek is followed all over the Malësi, and obeying its edicts, rather than being Christian or Muslim, is what makes you a Malësor, a highlander: important in a place which has almost always been under foreign dominion, whether Roman, Ottoman, or Serb. Even the modern age and the rule of Hoxha in Albania and Tito in Kosovo affected the Kanun remarkably little, since both dictators ensured their subjects had little choice but to stay in their mountain villages, and neither supplied good education or reliable neutral lawgivers. In fact, the communist emphasis on secularism, and the stripping away of the powers of the mosques and churches, probably encouraged a return to the values of the Kanun.

Men of the highlands are equal under the Kanun, which seems rather attractive and democratic until you realize that 'men' is racist and gendered. Only men born into a clan of Gheg descent are equal: everyone else is the enemy. Roma and Jews are a lower caste of humanity. Black people are lower still, though they have only theoretical existence for the Kanun, whereas there are – or were – many Roma, Serbs, Greeks, and a good sprinkling of Vlachs and Jews in the Malësi. Women exist only as men's property; they are 'sacks for carrying': carrying children, that is – also water, loads of wood, washing, crops for market, and large agricultural tools. Like a good sack, they should last as long as the man who owns them, or from the time they are douche bags to the time they are old bags, as we might put it in English. Women have 'long hair and short minds'. They have no right to speak to men or to enter a room in which men are talking. Men can have more than one wife. Wives can be replaced if they do not produce sons, killed if they prove false or betray hospitality, and beaten for idleness like any beast of burden. The Kanun also provides for their being stripped naked and driven through the village with a whip.

Marriages are long in the negotiation and the man pays an agreed bride price. This sum is the full value of the woman's life: once it is paid, the wife's family may take no revenge if the husband kills her – hence the wedding bullet. Women can only escape from this fate and take on responsibility for and ownership of their own lives if, under one of the most famously peculiar provisions of the Kanun, they become 'sworn virgins', vowing to be celibate forever and live as men, often in men's clothes. There is no provision for divorce: only repudiation.

The Kanun is ancient. Certainly, it predates Lek Dukagjin, who was probably trying to control and penalize traditional blood-taking when – or if – he codified the law. Similar systems must once have sustained the continent of Europe: we know of some in the Iceland of the Sagas, the Scottish Highlands, and the hill villages of Sicily. But the Kanun is not a tradition in the ornamental sense, like a Scottish skibo. It is antique, but it is alive: and alive not quaintly and rarely, like the duck-billed platypus, but commonly and effectively, like the crocodile, which has had little reason to change its horrifying design since the age of the dinosaurs. The Kanun is alive in my kitchen, in the person of Antigona, who was married with a bullet and beaten like a donkey. She grew up as a member of a *fis* – a clan – and saw justice administered by elders gathered in the manner prescribed by the Kanun, not occasionally but regularly. She was breastfed as a baby by several women of the *fis* besides her mother, and later passed her own babies to clanswomen for the same service. She knew several sworn virgins; also concubines; also men who took on a dead brother's wife; also couples promised in marriage while still in the womb. She knew dozens killed or wounded in blood feuds, and stayed up all night for a week with a brother injured in a vendetta, drawing pus from his shoulder with a turkey-baster.

The Kanun is extraordinarily detailed and interfering. It remembers the life of the Malësi, but also dictates it. It tells you how to mill corn and shoe a horse, as well as laying down the composition of a jury and monetary compensation payments for deaths. It is fiercely puritan and compulsively dirty-minded, prescribing the exhibition of sheets after a wedding night and special sleeping places for menstruating women. You would wonder how such an oppressive and conservative system could possibly continue, if it were not for the thrilling base freedoms it also grants.

For, at its core, the Kanun is not a system of law at all. Law takes the administration of justice away from the aggrieved and aggrieving parties and settles them according to some sort of rule, whether religious or democratic or even tyrannical. The Kanun of Lek, in contrast, returns the administering of justice to the families of the aggrieved. It caters to some of our most powerful instincts, the sort the tabloid papers howl for every time a paedophile comes to court – loyalty, love of family, revenge. It enshrines ideas of blood vengeance, honour, hospitality and atonement straight from the Bronze Age, and is easier to understand if you remember your Aeschylus and Euripides.

The Kanun says that you must open your house to strangers, and that host and guest become brothers, like Herakles and Admetus. The Kanun says that incest, up to and including marrying your fifth cousin five times removed, is a sin which must be atoned for with blood, like that of Oedipus. The Kanun says the stealing of a wife, even if the wife fully consents, like Helen of Troy, or even if she is a second wife, like Patroclus's handmaid, must be atoned for with the blood of her lover. The Kanun says the murder of a man stains all his male relatives, and that the stains can be only cleansed with more blood. The son or nephew or grandson or great-grandson is charged with the honour of the father, like Orestes, except that the Kanun's Furies are absolutely not walled up under the gates of a city, but freely roam the Malësi.

Actually, the Furies are having a ball. These are fat times. The Kanun of Lek has not been killed by television; it is available in several languages, in paperback, and over the Internet. The stultifying peace of communism lulled it a little, but now that the rule of Hoxha has given way to corruption and a legal vacuum in northern Albania, and the whole of the Malësi has been destabilized and freshly supplied with guns by the war on the Kosovan side, it has roared into new life. There is no church or mosque to hold it back: Albania is one of the few officially atheist countries in the world. The horrors of the war itself are much more comprehensible if you understand the workings of the Kanun. Lek strictly proscribed the killing of women by men outside their clan, but the killing of families in revenge for the deaths of men, the burning of houses and the sacking of villages – these are sanctions laid down in the Kanun: Bronze Age punishments meted out with mortars and guns.

In Albania today there are hundreds of boys who cannot go to school because their families are 'in blood' with another and they risk being shot. The building of traditional stockade houses has been revived in Kosovo and northern Albania, and one carpenter, for instance, has been hiding inside one for four years because he is 'in blood' with the family of a man who robbed him and then rode his bike into a power pylon while making his escape. Albanian men maintain their traditional right to have a gun. Highway robbery is flourishing. For this reason, the Foreign Office recommends that you do not visit northern Albania. Things have yet to reach the heights of the nineteenth century, when a blood feud which began over a single gun cartridge lead to the deaths of 132 men and the sacking of 1,218 houses in just two years, but it looks as if they are getting there.

The Kanun of Lek writes itself on the memories of all its citizens, and, like other viruses, is adaptable. It has learned to live outside its mountain fastnesses. Agim, for example, who has been living in Britain since 1998 and who has in that time paid all his taxes with fanatical zeal and has never incurred so much as a parking ticket, is 'in blood' with some Catholics in a neighbouring hamlet to his Kosovan village. A dispute about a bicycle, and one of them stabbed him with a screwdriver and he haemorrhaged and the doctors removed – his spleen, perhaps? The men with the screwdriver, of course, may not live in Kosovo any more. Maybe the Serbs burned their homes and killed their families in their own version of a vendetta. It will make no difference: Agim remembers the blood. It has not been atoned for, and so he carries the invisible, ancient stain with him all the time, even when driving his taxi and taking his wife round Primark.

I tell Antigona the story of the Oresteia. She listens to it keenly, freshly, as if it were now, as if I were telling tales of an odd neighbour. She understands Orestes' dilemma immediately, and thinks Clytemnestra a very dirty woman. She likes the Furies, too: she says they are just like her mother-in-law. I tell her I once saw the Oresteia staged with the principals in full Greek masks and padded boots, and the chorus as old Eastern European men in overcoats and stout old women in tight black dresses. The chorus lugged huge cauldrons around with them and muttered together, and poured out pot after pot of beetroot soup for the Furies, exactly the thick, textured purple of arterial blood.

Antigona is not familiar with beetroot. But she tells me a coda to the story of her dead sister and the magic papers. That was also part of a vendetta. Antigona's father's aunt had gone swimming with another teenage girl and the girl had drowned. So the girl's family set the curse of illness on Antigona's mother which was only averted by the sacrifice of the blonde baby. The baby was a good sacrifice because she was so very doted on. The death would be terribly painful for Antigona's family, sufficiently painful to cleanse the pain of the drowned teenager's family. Blood would wipe out blood, and the feud would end.

'But I think,' says Antigona, 'I think she caught her foot, that girl who drowned.' There are tears in her eyes. 'It's easy, when you're swimming, to catch your foot. It's muddy, you can't see the bottom, there are rocks.'

And we both think about it: the girl who drowned, her friend who walked home to tell everyone, the family who lost a daughter. Then we think about the child who died, a toddler no older than the doted-upon Sam, and about Antigona's mother waking from her illness to find her golden baby buried, because they inter bodies immediately in the Malësi and the mother was so very ill, burning and raving. Antigona brought water and her mother didn't recognize her. Antigona will always remember it.

We are folding bedclothes. We stop and sit on the bed and I mention freak currents, and we both say again how terribly hard it is to see the bottom of the river, how very easy to catch your foot and be pulled right under.

But the Kanun of Lek makes no allowance for mud, or for accidents, or for human weakness. I can't see how such a system can be sustainable. There is no space for changing your mind here, or for the immutable force of desire: no love matches, no adultery – don't such things happen, in the Malësi?

Oh yes. Often. For instance, Antigona's second cousin married a Roma boy. Her first cousin by marriage was impregnated at fourteen by an older man who was employing her in his fields. That girl's cousin married a Catholic. Another girl in Antigona's clan ran away from her arranged marriage with a man everyone knew was a trafficker. Still another got pregnant by a man she was not engaged to. Everyone knows about the girl who resisted her marriage and was sold by her brothers, her *brothers,* mark you, to a notorious trafficker and was forced into prostitution in Italy.

And then, what happened to them?

There is a sort of cliff and you fall off it. The lucky ones were ostracized. If they were still in the village when the sin was discovered, they were beaten, stripped and run out of town; if they weren't, they became bywords for shame. The cousin who married the Roma stayed ostracized. She has never had any contact with her family and that is twenty years ago now. The impregnated cousin was saved by a kind uncle, allowed to keep the baby, and even subsequently married, but she is stained: you can still tell she is a nasty sort of woman who probably sleeps with everyone. The one who married the Catholic was accepted back pretty quickly: after all, her husband adhered to the Kanun, he was still a good mountain man.

Or, they were killed. The cousin who ran away with the trafficker disappeared entirely and is presumed dead. The other girl who got pregnant was murdered – a pillow over the head – by her own family, probably her mother. The girl who was sold into prostitution escaped after a few years and made it home, and then her brothers shot her dead in the public square.

'That's terrible,' I say. 'It wasn't her fault.'

'Yes,' says Antigona. 'But she was prostitute, her brothers were shamed. You can't tell, if a woman is prostitute, those kind of dirty women, they sleep with lots of men, they start to enjoy it.'

But Antigona herself is divorced: she has fallen off the cliff. The Kanun makes no distinction between divorce and adultery: both generate shame which covers all the members of the woman's family and must be purged with violence. Agim, Driton and Hasan forced Antigona to bring Fazli to this country in order to avoid this shame, and she gave in because she understood that. When she eventually divorced Fazli all the same, they felt the stain, all the more strongly for the incomprehension around them. When she first met me, Antigona told me she was divorced at once in order to see if I would acknowledge her. She was both warning me off – because, under the Kanun, she was not just contaminated but a contaminate – and testing the new water, guessing that I would not see the stain. Because Antigona sees herself as clean.

'When I was young,' says Antigona, 'I was wild child but I was very clean. Always my clothes and everything – when I had my periods, no one knew, I washed out the – thingies – and dried them white, white, where no one saw. When my sisters left theirs out to dry and I saw them, and they weren't clean, white white, I picked them up and came running in the house and threw them at them – Disgusting! Disgusting.'

I'm getting the idea now, about the shame. It's like menstrual blood – the magic liquid that seeps out of women, whether they want it or not, the sticky, clotting stuff that makes them smell of beef and corpses, that greens and rusts clothes, that turns milk, that contaminates, that betrays them suddenly, on their white clothes.

Under the Kanun, men have to cleanse themselves of shame with fresh blood and clear the air with gunpowder, while women, it seems, just keep washing. This is why Antigona's war against dirt has a spiritual zeal about it. This is her honour, so she has to be vigilant, ever ready to pick up a broom and sweep dust out of the door, change a garment that has picked up a little grime. This why she wants me to join in conversations where we condemn other women's cleanliness. She is not trying to tell me I am dirty: I am her friend, and clean is a spiritual state. She is trying to keep me safe: you have to keep yourself safe from shame by passing the shame along, by making sure that someone else is the dirty one, someone else will be hounded out of the village. And if you are a clean woman, you have to demonstrate it; you have to confront dirty women with their dirty rags. You have to keep throwing the dirt out of the house. You have to put the rubbish where it belongs.

So now Antigona is a professional cleaner; she is hiring out her zeal.

What does she find under our beds? Dirty tights, Lego bricks, knickers, small socks, plastic cars, pens, the *LRB*, the *TLS*, page proofs, scrumpled hankies, bills, small change, and once (not in my house) a used condom. But not the sensational stuff out of soap operas, or from the imagination of Fazli, who often accused Antigona of having sex with all her employers, male and female: not fluffy handcuffs, corsets, or billets-doux, never hidden credit card bills and incriminating phone numbers. Our dirt doesn't mean that, exactly. I don't know many marriages haunted by adultery; I didn't know anyone fixated by promiscuity until I met those who grew up under the Kanun of Lek.

But our dirt is not empty of meaning. Often, the long skeins of dust are the fruit of an ongoing wrangle about time and status: about which partner has a gap in her schedule long enough to sweep under the bed, and which partner thinks his job is too important for him to sweep under the bed. The toys speak of arguments, spoken or unspoken, about which parent is more intensely involved with the kids – the boring stuff!

day-to-day constant care! – and therefore does not have time to sweep under the bed; and which parent is always getting all the paints and cars out and never puts them back and lets the kids stuff everything under the bed. And in the darkest corners lurk unmentionable, soiled arguments about who does not ever even look under the bed because his mother brought him up wrong, the sexist pig; and who doesn't give a stuff about under the bed, and since when did you care about under the bed, and how can we be so petty as to be even talking about this. Which is when many of us hired Antigona or someone like her. She papers over the holes in our lengthily negotiated, self-conscious, hopeful marriages; the question of who would do the wife's work, the drudgery. She sweeps up under the bed.

I don't know how much of this Antigona understands: after all, it is all rather peculiar and culturally specialized. All dirt is still, in her view, a woman's fault: she will rush in horror to remove a dishcloth or a nappy from my husband's hand, and I am certain she gossips about our house to her Albanian friends. On the other hand, she often admires the conversations she hears between partners: calm, lengthy discussions of children or of a day's events. She watches my husband play with Sam with frank envy. And she was very struck when my friend Jeannie's husband said to her after a huge domestic mix-up, 'We can't say whose fault it was because we decided not to. We don't blame each other. Whatever happens, we don't do blame.'

'No blame,' repeats Antigona. She is scouring the

steel sink, with which I think she is unnecessarily obsessed. She leans back to contemplate the sheen and raises her eyebrows right to her hairline, as if admiring some vast, outlandish work of art. 'That's nice, innit?'

My friend Anu from Finland comes to stay. She knows a lot about Albania – but then, every Finn I have ever met is supernaturally well informed about everything. We get to this conversation:

'What I don't understand,' I say, 'is this. Albania, right. Large country, really rough terrain, not many natural resources, small population, weird language, oral culture until recently, terrible history of being part of different empires all the time, terrible time in the war – you can see how that ends up in a real mess. You can see why the women get oppressed. Except, you know, that's the history of Finland too. And the geography. But Finland is the most feminist place on earth, and the most literate, whichever way you measure it.'

'And has great design values,' says Anu.

'How do you account for it?'

'I think about that a lot,' says Anu, whose family fled from Karelia during the horrors of the Russian war, and whose grandmother can tell refugee stories to match Antigona's. 'Why? What was it that happened to us, a civil war – the Russians on the border – what's the recipe?'

'Because I don't believe in national character – it is such sentimental rubbish – football commentator chatter.'

'It's fascism,' says Anu, very seriously. 'Of course,

the Albanians are our equals. I think maybe – the weather?'

As part of my research project, I start to read Antigona Edith Durham's *High Albania*, an account of the Malësi in 1908, bit by bit, over lunch. She is very taken with it, delighted with the way the century-old account describes her former life so accurately. Traditional costume of felt dress over baggy trousers with studded belt, even when the temperature is in the nineties? Not only her mother but also her older sister dressed like that. Greased-in ringlets combed forward and sewn with little brass bells to the collar? Catholics only – but they're still at it. Two-storey house with the second storey as a sort of parlour for the men to do business in? Wells, springs, open fires? Check, check, and definitely check. Antigona plans never to clean such a parlour again, and never to live without a washing machine. We get to this story:

THE TALE OF THE MAN WHO COULD UNDERSTAND BEASTS AND BIRDS

A certain man was gifted with the power to understand the talk of beasts and birds. But on condition only that, should he ever tell that which he heard, he would drop down dead . . .

But his wife was wicked as all women are . . . and all day and all night she gave him no peace . . . for still she asked: 'What did the donkey say?'

Worn out at last, he could bear no more: 'Tomorrow I will tell you . . .'

So the poor man went out to take a last look at his yard, and there he saw the cock standing on tiptoe, flapping his wings and crowing as loud as he could . . . 'I shall die of laughing! Look at him – the silly fool! He has only one wife, and cannot manage her; while I have fifty, and keep them all in order!'

The man heard this. He picked up a large stick, and went back into the house. 'Do you want to know what the donkey said?' he asked. 'Yes,' said his wife. Then he gave her a good beating. 'Do you want to know what the donkey said?' he asked. 'Yes,' said she. So he beat her again. 'Do you want to know what the donkey said?' 'Yes,' said she. So a third time he beat her till he was quite tired. 'Do you still want to know what the donkey said?' 'No,' said she, and they lived very happily ever afterwards.

Yes, Antigona knows that story. It's one of many. If a man doesn't beat his wife in the Malësi, if his wife rules, then people say he has changed heads with a donkey. You see, the donkey story shows an acceptable level of beating. The wife is being very unreasonable, so she needs beating, and you will notice she can still talk, even after the third attack, so the husband is being moderate and correct. I tell her about Titania and Bottom, and, thinking about the cock in the story, explain the word 'henpecked', which makes her laugh.

Antigona explains that Fazli's beatings went beyond

what is acceptable in the Kanun of Lek. You aren't supposed to beat your wife bloody: if you do, she may complain to her parents, and you have to give an explanation. But Fazli's beatings carried on after Agim went round with the Kalashnikov, they went on despite the sympathy of even Antigona's sisters-in-law and father-in-law, they went on after Antigona several times tried to run away. Fazli was usually drunk when he beat her; he aimed for the head.

I say I don't think there much point in a law which allows you to beat a wife sometimes; you really need to say, no beating.

But in the Malësi, Antigona says, if a man doesn't beat his wife, they say she has fed him donkey brain. Or that she has put menstrual blood in his food. A sour, dark expression has come over her face. I try to lighten the mood.

'Sounds like a good idea,' I say. 'Did you try it?'

'Don't be stupid,' spits Antigona. 'What difference would that have made – a donkey's brain?'

Antigona is given to these bursts of disconcerting worldliness. She thinks there are plenty of gay men in the Malësi, for example, but that they hide it, which 'makes them worse'. And she says some sworn virgins are 'just born like that. Like Amelia.' Amelia is my good lesbian friend, and I have never mentioned her orientation. I don't think these slips into cynicism are new since she came to England, either. I think they give an indication of how people live with a code as puritan as the Kanun; how they have affairs, let things slip, turn a blind eye, how one day someone will mention donkey brain and everyone will laugh, brew another cup of coffee, and feel better.

When her sister Blerta's husband first raised his hand to her, Blerta thumped him back with the large pestle she used to do the washing, and after that they got on very well. There are many happy couples in the Malësi, says Antigona. Men who just hit their wives sometimes, when they need it.

Antigona adapts, she changes: it is one of the markers of her great intelligence. Over the six years I know her, her English improves until she can make NTL or Hackney Council back down, or, more to the point, deliver her judgements and jokes in the full stinging irony with which they were conceived. She learns the language of clothes, too: never 'understated', true, but certainly 'chic', 'sleek', 'ladylike', 'Sophia Loren'. She influences me: I am distinctly less baggy and scruffy. We learn to buy each other presents we actually like, from Zara.

But Antigona never learns to rub along with the Kanun. Instead, she fights it, in sudden ambushes and grim, furious rearguard actions, the way she taunts imaginary Imams with pork sausages; the way, I am sure, she fought Fazli and her mother-in-law; the way I will later watch her fight her daughters. She goes to work as a waitress, daring the disapproval of her brothers, relishing the public exposure. She never does settle for any sort of actual relationship with a man, but she always maintains her terrific appearance and flirts ruthlessly. She always has at least one hanger-on, a man on the phone to ask her for coffee or send her texts, or, in the case of the owner of the Italian delicatessen and the adviser in the CAB (!), to propose marriage. 'Nothing to be embarrassed 'bout, hey?' she will say, when picking up the phone or going into town for 'one coffee', though it is certainly not my disapproval she is daring.

I do disapprove, though, when she sees the Kanun peering from under the veils of local Muslim women, and vents her rage on them. The years Antigona spends here, 2000–6, are the years our always traditional, inward-looking Bangladeshi and Pakistani communities suffer a sudden increase in suspicion from the outside world, and new fundamentalist pressures from within: these are the post 9/11 years, the niqāb years, and it makes Antigona furious. She is not interested in questions of faith: she sees Shame at work on these women, who, because they are immigrants, are reflections of her. She feels Shame bouncing back to her, and she spits it out.

'When I see a fat Pakistani lady in her car, and she is in the car because she is ashamed to walk, and she look at me like, "You should be shamed," cos I am dressed like this, and walking on the road, and she is wearing scarf, long dress thingy, well, I look back at her like *you* should be shamed. And' – she starts to giggle – 'when it catches in the car door, I laugh and laugh.'

Of course, I argue with her. I tell her she can't expect to escape racist treatment then dole it out herself. I remind her of her past, tell her she should have more sympathy. 'But they live here!' responds Antigona. 'They can go the police, refuge, benefits, single mum, all this! They do not need to live like that.'

Three years after her arrival, there is an honour killing just four streets away from us. A Kurdish woman caught planning an elopement is strangled by, it seems, her brothers acting on their mother's instructions. Antigona is fixated by this event, poring over all the reports, staring over the police cordon round the house, peering in at the window. She talks about it to everyone, full of condemnation for the family, for Muslims in general, for the way 'they' treat their daughters.

'Did that happen in the Malësi?' I asked. 'A killing like that, I mean, that you remember?'

'Of course it did!' says Antigona. 'There was a girl I knew, she had two sisters, she got a boyfriend, the sisters, they got jealous ['jealous' is Antigona's word for honour-rage. She uses it for vendettas, too]. They think they will not have husbands, they kill her. In bed. You know, with pillow. Then they have the funeral. They say accident. But everyone know.'

'Well, what did you think then?'

'Then – I was frightened, actually. Because I tried to run away from my marriage. I think – maybe they do that to me.'

'Well, maybe the women in those communities, that mother, maybe she was scared like that?'

'Then she is crazy. Her daughter, she was university student! This is England! I hope she go to prison actually, that Mum. That'll teach her. Good long stretch.'

'That'll teach her', 'Good long stretch'. These are not Antigona's phrases. She has been working on this judgement, rehearsing it at Toddler Group and the Drop-In Centre, practising her role as the Western woman who knows nothing of the Kanun of Lek, who thinks it can be locked up or rooted out.

When Ylli has his first swimming lesson with his school he returns with reports of Muslim girls and even some of the boys swimming in 'pyjamas'.

'Why the school let them?' demands Antigona. 'It is disgusting! Pyjamas in the water!'

'Otherwise the girls wouldn't be allowed to swim.'

'That one is not true! If the school say, OK, no pyjamas, then 99 per cent, they not wear pyjamas. But if the school not say it, and one girl she wear pyjamas, then her mum say to the other mums, my girl is in pyjamas, your girl should be ashamed, innit?'

Antigona's nose for shame is better than mine. Nevertheless, it is my job to argue. 'In France they have that rule,' I say. 'No hijab in school, no turban, and it works out worse. It generates more violence. More problems in the future.'

'But,' says Antigona, 'why she have to cover her body? She is not woman! Why she have to wear scarf to school? She is seven years old. She want to run and jump. She is child. She should not be shamed.'

She knows that will silence me. Because isn't that what I've told her from the start, from the first time she held out her hand to me, telling me she was dee-vorced, dee-vorced: that she has nothing to be ashamed of, that she should not be shamed?

'Thanks God my mother beat me up,' says Antigona. 'If she didn't, I could never manage when my husband beat me.'

'Why did your mother beat you?'

'I was wild. Wild child. I liked to climb trees. All the things the boys do, I do them better.'

I imagine a ten-year-old Antigona, bright-eyed and tensile, hanging by her heels from a branch.

'I always love my Mum, even when she slap me. It makes me strong.'

I never challenge Antigona on this mantra, but I also entrust her with my baby, and never for a moment doubt that she will lay any but the most tender of touches on her. It is one of the many impossible contradictions she lives with. You cannot be brought up in a code like the Kanun, a code built on the overwhelming emotions we call 'gut feeling', without feeling them in your guts. We take our laws and customs into our bodies: my bowels freeze in a Chinese lavatory because there are no doors; my husband has a Taiwanese PhD student who cannot stop bowing, even though he is exquisitely attuned to Western mores and knows it is not culturally appropriate. In her head, Antigona believes in a version of the Declaration of Human Rights as explained to her by me, *EastEnders* and her lawyer. In her guts, Antigona believes that love is violent. With her head, she rejects the shame of the Kanun of Lek, but her body feels it. The Kanun is not finished with its work on Antigona just because she has left her husband, crossed a border. The Kanun is biding its time, sucking its pink gums, doing a little quiet knitting in the shadow behind the guillotine.

4
How She Left Him

Things I Know How to Do and Antigona Doesn't: No. 3

TAKE PAINKILLERS

Paracetamol, aspirin, ibuprofen, in their generic and commercial wrappings: I know them all. Antigona is chary of them, feeling either that it is letting down her Highlander pride to need them, or that her body will somehow, being foreign, not react properly to them. But she gets headaches, terrible headaches, and gut ache, and menstrual ache, and when she discovers the dent my pills can make in them, she is delighted, particularly with Nurofen, and later, with the information that you can take it alongside paracetamol.

When we sit at the kitchen table and I shove across the sugar-coated pills and say, 'You can take three but I wouldn't go for four,' or reach down the Migraleve and check the back to see if you can have aspirin alongside, Antigona sometimes remembers the blows she has suffered, and tells me. She tells me more about bruises when I can't teach her to ride my bike, for all our trying, and when I recommend my kind GP and she comes back with counsel and iron pills.

Things Antigona Knows How to Do and I Don't: No. 3

KEEP WORKING WHILE IN ACUTE PHYSICAL PAIN

I have no idea how that is done. But I know Antigona kept hoeing, harrowing, gathering, washing, cooking, childrearing and childbearing through all the blows that fell on her. She had no choice.

Selective Inventory of Injuries Inflicted on Antigona by her Husband, in Roughly Chronological Order

Bruises
Half a front tooth.
Bruises Black Eye.
Injury to windpipe resulting from a throttling during which Antigona's tongue was forced out of her mouth and her nose bled. Antigona able only to whisper for one month.
Bruises Black eye Cracked ribs.
Nameless injury resulting from rape while still bleeding from first birth.
Two more front teeth.
Black eye Bruises Black eye Bruises Black eye.
Broken jaw.
Other half of first tooth.

Black eye Bruises Black eye Bruises Black eye Bruises Black eye Bruises Black eye Cracked ribs.

Miscarriage induced: three-month pregnancy. Blood, so much blood.

Remaining front teeth.

Bruises Bruises Bruises Black eye Bruises Bruises Black eye Bruises Black eye Cracked ribs Bruises Bruises.

Injury to hip bone – Antigona unable to walk properly for two months.

Black eye Bruises Black eye Bruises Black eye Cracked ribs Bruises Bruises Black eye Bruises Bruises Black eye Bruises Bruises.

Miscarriage induced: six-month pregnancy, boy foetus.

Black eye Bruises Black eye Bruises Black eye Bruises Black eye Bruises Black eye Cracked ribs Bruises Bruises Black eye Bruises Black eye Cracked ribs Bruises.

Ad nauseam . . .

Over the years, too, Antigona tells me the story of her marriage and divorce. When I meet her, her decree nisi is nearly in the post – divorce is relatively simple when there are no papers and no property – but it is another two years before Fazli is finally deported from Britain. During that time, I gradually come to understand more about the Kanun of Lek, and Antigona understands more both about what divorce means in England, and about what her divorce has meant for her. We go over the story of her marriage and her leaving of it over and over again: she always wants to talk about it; she grows more and more proud of it. We fashion the narrative together; we reinforce it with praise and understanding and polish for particular episodes until it becomes a shining thing. When people express an interest in Antigona – they always do – I tell them the outline of this story to bait them, have them asking for more. It always works. Antigona does the same thing: I hear her at it, with the hardbitten mums in the school playground, with the kindly pierced workers at the Drop-In. We all like it because it reflects well on all of us: it is feminism and liberal democracy at their finest. It starts with a But.

BUT

Nevertheless. However. Despite Tradition, Opinion, and the Kanun of Lek:

Here in England, men are not allowed to kill their wives. They are not allowed to hit them. They are not even allowed to rape them. Excellent laws, put in place by single-minded, difficult women who would not take 'no' for an answer, and whom we don't celebrate often enough. And, over the first nine months of Antigona's life in London, the difference steadily seeped in on her.

By then the family, including Fazli, was settled in the little house in my street. This was when I first used to observe them walking by, and Antigona also observed me, pale and frightened with my new pushchair, but not often, because she was too busy. Antigona was paying back her brothers for her passage by working in a sweet factory during the day and cleaning a pizza restaurant at night. 'Working like a cow,' she says – the sort of bludgeoning hard labour which silences most women, makes them wall-eyed and stupid.

Not Antigona. She was not speaking English well yet, but she understood more every day. Her daughters were rapidly acquiring the language – Flora was a star pupil, and would get an 'A' at GCSE English after just eighteen months in this country. And there was the television. Antigona loved the soaps – so like her own life in their drastic, melodramatic turns. She especially liked the look of policemen as they appeared on these series: solid, pallid Plods, smiling Asian women – very different from the Italians who had humiliated her. She thought they looked kind, actually. She thought she might call them up.

Fazli himself had no job, of course. He had got himself fired from Agim's factory and Driton's factory and Antigona's pizza restaurant. He was drinking all day and gambling all night and vice versa, and beating up Antigona more than ever. Agim and Driton had seen her bruises and black eyes, and though they didn't exactly say sorry, they did go round and shout at Fazli a few times. Antigona, with her usual optimism, began to think they would not reject her if she left him. Fazli beat up the girls too, especially Mihane, when they tried to defend their mother.

EastEnders ran a story about wife-beating. Antigona watched the whole procedure: the calling of the police, the visit to the sympathetic lawyer, the 'hanging's too good for him' reaction of the fictional community. The woman was not shamed. 'Nothing to be ashamed of, love,' characters endlessly repeated. The phrase arrived in her head, miraculously clear.

She began to speak to her co-workers. 'Your husband is here again,' they often said, and when she looked out of the window, there would be Fazli, jumping up and down in the car park to get a view through the window. Later in the evening, he would berate her and beat her for sharing a table with a black guy, or speaking to an Algerian woman. 'I wouldn't put up with that,' said the white woman opposite. 'You call the police, love.'

In September of 2001, Antigona went to the NHS dentist and got a whole set of new teeth. Fazli always grabbed her wages straight from the packet, never missed a payday, so she got money for the teeth from Agim, and kept some of it aside. With the cash, she secretly bought a mobile phone from the pawnshop. She charged it up, she got credit for it. And the next time Fazli came home drunk and thumped her, she pulled all the children up into her bedroom, and got the phone from its hiding place.

It is four in the morning. They push the bed against the door and lean on it, all four of them. Antigona dials 999. Ylli is sobbing. His Daddy is telling him to come out to him, to be a good boy and open the door. Ylli is four now. He goes to the school over the road, but his glorious confidence has been knocked by the transition from Italian. The only English word he will say is 'sorry'. He is saying it now, to the bedclothes. His Daddy is banging again, cracking the plywood of the cheap hollow door, shoving the bed steadily back into the room. Antigona gets through, but at the same moment so does Fazli, and Antigona's English fails her, leaving her gibbering into the phone. Fazli grabs the phone and pulls out the SIM card, and throws both away. Then he starts on Antigona's face.

Mihane pulls the phone under the bedcovers, then darts out a hand, grabs the SIM card, and tucks it back in place. Seconds later, the police ring back and she calmly gives their full address. No one hears her do this, because Fazli is throwing Antigona against a wall. Then Mihane lies flat on the mattress, the phone under her stomach, and tries to make herself an invisible bump of candlewick bedspread.

It must have been a quiet night for the law, because the police turned up minutes later, flattened the door, rushed up the stairs, and charged into the bedroom just in time to see Fazli grab Flora by the throat and bash her head against the wall. They arrested him and took him away in a patrol car. Mihane and Ylli watched him go from the upstairs window, his hands locked behind his back. A kindly policewoman made them tea and asked a lot of questions. Then she went away.

The children crawled into Antigona's bed and went to sleep. Antigona got in with them and studied her bedroom door. It was sagging sadly from its twisted hinge, but for the first time in seventeen years there was no possibility of Fazli coming through it to beat her again. Dawn was coming, one of those damp grey English dawns which hardly seem to take place at all. In an hour or two she would be out in the glorious, indifferent street, walking past people who knew nothing of the Kanun of Lek, people who might even be divorced themselves, people who might not look at her, but would certainly not condemn her.

The main problem with domestic violence cases, any police officer will tell you, isn't arresting the bastards in the first place; it's getting the women to follow through. You can have the case all sewn up, hospital reports, photos, the works, and then the guy will go round and wheedle away and before you know it, she's withdrawn the charges, he's moved back in, and a load of police hours have gone up in smoke. Then you start the whole procedure again, six months later. When I taught in a sixth-form college, I had a student, Janine, whose mother had been leaving her violent stepfather in this way for fifteen years. The first thing the police did the next day, and the next, was to check if Antigona still wanted to press charges.

But she did. She was photo-perfect: calm, bruised, lucid, unwavering. And just as good the day after that. In fact, she soon became a pet case for the domestic violence unit, a model pupil. She went for the whole package: charges, divorce, and an injunction for Fazli never to come within 150 feet of her. She remained flinty as, over the next three years, he broke injunctions not to harass or approach Antigona on fourteen separate occasions; he was arrested for being drunk and disorderly, twice; for driving without a licence, twice; for driving drunk without a licence, once; and for threatening a nightclub bouncer with a knife. She resisted his impassioned pleas for help as his appeals to remain in the country were serially rejected; even when he was, like Hasan, locked up in Dover, and Flora, Ylli, and Mihane went down to see him. Few women in her position manage so well.

But most women in Antigona's position are, or were, in love. The men who beat them and abase them also once elevated and adored them. Beating and forgiveness may well be a central coil of their relationship. Not Antigona. She never lay voluntarily in Fazli's arms; she never, as far as she can remember, even had a pleasant conversation with him.

She certainly never courted him. She didn't even have the grace of a long-arranged marriage with a family known to her; the peeking at each other, perhaps, as children, round the long tables of someone else's wedding feast; the honour of a high bride-price or an elaborate, expensive wedding ceremony. It was all too bottom-rung: Antigona was the third daughter of a poor man, and her older sisters, Blerta and Jehona, were married at the same time. She was also, she says, 'pretty and things': her looks, which were and are of the sort called 'bombshell' or 'firecracker', were causing rumours in the village. She was the end of a job lot, explosive stock with an expiry date. A bargain basement offer came in from the uncle with the telly.

Antigona resisted from the start. She didn't like her corrupt uncle. She knew fine well he was having an affair with Fazli's mother. She loved her mother, she loved her village, she wanted to make her own choice of husband. Nevertheless, she didn't quite say 'no', because she wanted to please her mother. So she was deemed to be engaged to Fazli. This meant that when he was brought round to her village for a look-see and she immediately decided he was a prize idiot and nasty into the bargain, she was breaking her engagement. Under the Kanun, this only gives you one option.

'Why didn't you try to be a sworn virgin?' I ask. I think it sounds rather romantic and magnificent. There is a picture of one in my Edith Durham book, barefoot and smoking on a rock. Antigona soon puts me in my place.

Because her brothers were alive! Sworn virgins are for when there aren't any brothers. She already had three brothers, they didn't need another man in the family with inheritance rights. Besides.

Besides what?

Antigona is tight-lipped and angry. I wouldn't understand. There were huge family rows. Shamings. The whole family gathered to shout at her, night after night. She was covering them with disgrace. Then it all went quiet, and a cousin said, 'You are going to marry him.'

'Why?'

'You've been eating the soup.'

The family had been to the Imam for another spell. This time, the magic paper had been powdered into Antigona's soup. Now she'd have to marry Fazli, she'd see.

The next day, her uncle put her in his van. She thought her Mum was going, too, but the doors shut and they rattled off over the mountains, Antigona in the dark in the back, unable to see where they were going. They arrived at Fazli's house in the evening, Antigona was taken in, and before she was even offered a piece of bread, Fazli took her into his room and raped her. Now she couldn't be a sworn virgin because she wasn't a virgin. She couldn't be a daughter any more, either. She could be a dirty woman, she could be ostracized, she could slide down the rapid slide which ends in being shot in the public square, or she could be Fazli's wife, living in Fazli's parents' house which was poorer than her own, subject to the whims of Fazli's shrewish mother and lazy sisters.

My Dad used to take me to restaurants, and put me on the table, and everyone would talk to me and laugh. And he used to take me driving. He had a car. I miss him. (Ylli)

He is still my Dad. And I loved my grandma. His mum. (Flora)

I didn't want him to, like, be deported. I just wanted him to stop hitting us. (Mihane)

You have to understand, I am with Antigona in all of this. I have no proper view of Fazli; I have never even seen all of him, just his jeans and boots outside our basement window and his heavy shoulders and brush of black hair from our upstairs bedroom, and on both of those occasions he was menacing us and I was spying for Antigona and desperate not to be spotted. Otherwise, I know him only from Antigona's and

Flora's accounts, and from transcripts of a court case in which he did not distinguish himself. So when I try to see the marriage from his point of view, I mostly fail.

But if I try – well, Fazli was a drunk, so he must have had a small view of himself, at bottom. And a gambler – so he must have had a desperate, hopeful streak. And he beat up his children, so he probably had been beaten himself as a child. He was twenty when he was married, with no known talents or looks or money or prospects. I imagine he thought Antigona was very beautiful, because she is, and I imagine he found the initial rejection very shaming. I also think she probably *looked through him*, something I have often been accused of myself and which I understand to be very bad for the male libido. I imagine Fazli looked at Antigona with awe and desire and saw her elegant cat-like jaw raised in defiance, and her marvellous wide-spaced black eyes gone diamond hard as they do when she is threatened, and instead of thinking that she was frightened or unhappy, thought that she saw into his miserable ashamed heart, and hit her.

A fortnight after the rape, they put a borrowed wedding dress on Antigona and she sat in the house and received company for three days. To Antigona's lasting regret, there are no photographs of this occasion, but Antigona assures me she looked very beautiful indeed and that all the neighbours expressed the view that Fazli was very lucky to marry so much above himself. A week later, he beat her up for the first time, and within the month she realized she was pregnant.

*

I've only touched two men who beat their wives. The first was my student Janine's stepdad, who was living back at home after a spell in prison. He came in to a meeting about money, about a grant for Janine to pay for books. He was thin and greasy and he wore a cheap suit, his manners were ingratiating and overbearing and he was disgustingly blatant in his eagerness to get his hands on the cash. My Head of Department, Frank, handled him with unmoved aplomb and got exactly the deal we wanted for Janine. At the end of the meeting the wife-beater shook hands with us. When we walked back into the staffroom, Frank wiped his hands on the tweedy armchair and shook them off and I followed suit.

When Antigona's downstairs neighbour started beating her teenage daughter, Antigona marched into their flat swinging Ylli's bike chain from one hand. She told the woman to stop, and she did. She got the girl off the floor. She said it didn't matter what the girl had done, the mother must stop, and the mother did. The girl was fourteen and pregnant, the mother said. The girl shouldn't be shamed, said Antigona, no matter. No one should beat her.

My other wife-beater was a classical musician, and I actually once shared a sauna with him. When his wife told us, we ostracized him, but this is of very limited effectiveness in London. We did not shame him, as I think when I hear him on the radio (very often now; he is getting famous, much more famous than his ex-wife, also a musician), gleaming through the orchestra his clean, plangent notes.

*

The day after she called the police, Antigona got up and went to work. In the evening, Agim, Driton, and Hasan came round. They came in, which was a good sign. Agim took Ylli on his knee and bounced him, which was even better, and they accepted coffee brewed by Flora, which was tantamount to full acceptance. Nothing explicit was said until, after an hour, they rose to leave and Agim said Antigona might do as she wished about Fazli. Antigona said he would never cross her threshold again, and he didn't.

Agim's sister is a huge challenge for him. Agim has coped with the reversals of his life and the chaos of London by looking back, by drawing on the strengths of the Malësor: honour and pride and family. He has created, with his wife Era, a small Malësi in the tiny house in Clissold Park. He took over the place from the Council as an ex-squatted, hard-to-let property, and has more or less rebuilt it wall by wall. Now the house is fanatically clean and features faux-leather sofas with heart-shaped cushions: Era had some sort of 'Bad War', and the cleaning and the sofas seem to make her calm. She finds it very hard to leave the house, though. Agim's brothers are installed there too, under his command, in bunks in the box room. When Antigona and her family stayed there as well, the Christmas of the grimy hostel, they were crowded but oddly happy. They all knew where they were.

But Agim now often doesn't know where his sister is, and he cannot resist phoning her to find out. She is loose in what he sees as a very dangerous world. She keeps walking into strangers' houses, taking the family honour, which is his blood, his life, with her. When he accepted that she was going to be divorced, and yet that she would remain his sister, that he was not going to ostracize her or shoot her, he broke with the Kanun just as she did. The problem for him is that the Kanun holds him together, and he will find the break almost impossible to sustain.

For Antigona, though, the effects of leaving Fazli were beyond what she had ever imagined. She found herself full of energy and all sorts of new ideas. Within a few months of Fazli's departure, she stopped work at the restaurant and told the boss of the sweet factory who wanted her papers to 'go fuck himself, 'scuse my language', both of which cheering phrases she had recently acquired. Soon, she met me on the street corner and embarked on a new and much more profitable career cleaning houses.

Over the years, the ripples of the act spread well beyond herself. In the closed village of East London's Albanian community, Antigona became famous. First: she is the only Albanian woman anyone has heard of who actually used the British courts to divorce her husband. Second: she is unbowed, and, as the years go by, she only grows richer and stronger. She learns to drive, she keeps a lovely house, she visibly has good employment and counts middle-class Englishwomen as her friends. She is a figure of gossip and scandal, but none of it sticks. Year by year she becomes a powerful symbol to other Albanian women, and a threat to the men. Both frequently end up on her doorstep.

There is Lindita, for instance, whose children were taken away by Social Services because their father was beating them up so badly. If Lindita would leave her husband, she could have her children back. Here is Afrodita ringing the bell at midnight: her husband beats her up for using her mobile phone. Here is Flutura, come round to vent her feelings about her adulterous husband, and, hot on her heels, the man himself, threatening Antigona with hellfire and damnation. Ella says her husband has to have a mistress because she is not sexy enough on her own. 'How do you know you're not as sexy as his tart? Have you had a threesome?' shouts Antigona across the toddler group. 'You are not the problem. The problem is, he is a dog!' And one day, all the way from Naples, here is Pina, run away because her husband has mortgaged the bar and spent the money on his girlfriend.

All these women go back to their husbands: Lindita's children are permanently adopted, Afrodita puts up with the adulterer, so does Ella. Pina gives her husband another chance. Antigona is never angry with them, and always opens the door the next time. 'You have to be strong to walk out,' she says. 'Like me.'

But all our approval: mine, the lawyer's, the police's, all the sympathetic Englishwomen in their various hues, can't really compensate for the ambiguous attitude of Antigona's own family. The truce with her brothers after she threw out Fazli didn't last long. The Christmas of the grimy hostel and the near-disaster of Hasan brought the family together. But one afternoon in the spring after Hasan's return, on her way from one job to another, Antigona stopped in the park to chat with her employer's student lodger, out larking with a fluffy dog and a frisbee. She patted the dog and the young man showed her how to throw the frisbee. Antigona loves things like this: she has huge reserves of untapped athletic ability. In seconds, she had the frisbee hovering over the grass, the dog going bananas – when Hasan, out mooching, spotted her from the opposite path.

He rushed home to tell Agim. Agim summoned Antigona. She came with her children. The brothers sat on the slippery sofa, Antigona stood before them. Era, heavily pregnant, puffing, tried to gather the children into the kitchen, but they kept peering over her arm. Solemnly, Agim accused her of having an affair with the student. Hasan proudly produced his evidence. Antigona was first incredulous, then furious. She screamed, they screamed. Mihane and Flora burst in and screamed and tore their hair. Era screamed. Antigona was thrown out of the house onto the pavement with her children. Agim slammed the door.

There. There was shame and they have expelled it. The brothers felt better, purged. Antigona was on the pavement with her children. She wiped their faces. She wiped her own face. They got on the bus.

It was going to be all right, in fact. Driton would appear by her side in a day or two, smiling his silent sweet smile, and drive her to Tesco. He was acquiring some new ideas. He had met a Spanish girl, and intended to marry her. Her EU papers and her flat would allow him to slip from his brother's control. Era would have her baby, a girl, and need help. Antigona would come round and be invaluable. The row would be forgotten, then repeated, and repeated again.

But Antigona didn't know that just then. She sat and looked at the English rain, and the English people she did not understand, and back at her own children whom she must rear entirely alone. Her face was drained of all colour, sunk in a flat mask. She was feeling shame, and rage, and deep injustice, and also terribly lonely, the way pioneers must often do.

THE STORY OF THE CUCKOO

All this time, Antigona has had no idea what has happened to the rest of her family. Her mother and father, her older sisters Blerta and Jehona and her younger sister Vera, and their three husbands and their nine children. Alban, Djon, Mersela: I am learning their names. Agim has satellite TV, from Albania. There are many programmes to reunite the missing, but nothing about their family. There were mass slaughters and mass graves around the villages where their sisters were living. Antigona tells me this story:

'There was a girl whose family died. All her family: her mum, her dad, her brothers and sisters, everyone. Maybe they were killed in a war – I don't know. But she feel so sad, she cry all the time, and she say, I just want to change into a bird, and then she did change into a bird – that one she say cuck-oo.'

'The bird who lays her eggs in other birds' nests?'

'That one. She has no family, no one to help her, so

she can't keep her own children, so she put her children with other birds, and she cry.'

'Because, in the Malësi, the worst thing is not to have a family.'

'Yes. And we have a saying. Someone says, "Are you OK?" And if you are really down, you say, I'm lonely, lonely like a cuckoo.'

5

Pastoral: A Collection of All the Other Things Antigona Knows How to Do and I Don't

Over the years, I make a list of these because: they are beautiful – ingenious, hand-smoothed vestiges of the recent past, elegant as antique tools. They should be archived.

I make a list of them because: I worry that this is the knowledge of the future; that when, in order to save the planet, we settle down to carbon rations, we will also need to learn smallholding.

I make a list because: even though I believe the above, I am too squeamish, lazy and cack-handed actually to acquire any of this knowledge.

I do it because: writing is the thing that I know how to do and Antigona doesn't.

Things Antigona Knows How to Do and I Don't

NO. 4: SHEAR

Rosie and Jim, Sam's favourite TV programme, is a sort of hunt for redundant technologies: barge travel, hand-brickmaking. One day we all settle down to a particularly satisfying episode: 'Wool'. A sheep is sheared and emerges pinkly from its rug.

'Can you do that?' I ask Antigona.

'Yeah,' she says, as flatly as if I'd asked her if she could wash dishes, 'but not with that – machine.'

'The electric clippers?'

'Yeah. We did it just with knife. With knife in the hand. The sheep don't mind, actually.'

NO. 5: SPIN

Next up on the video, thread spooling from a wheel. 'Did you do that too?'

'Yeah. But not with that – thingy.'

'Not with that spinning wheel of seventeenth-century design?'

'No. No – that would be good. We wished for one like that.' (I'm momentarily reminded of *Monty Python*'s Yorkshiremen.) 'No. Just twist. Just twist in the hand. I hate that.'

Antigona touches her sleeve. 'You see this top?'

Matalan. £3.99. The quality: incredible. Antigona's

face shines with the joy of one who will never have to spin again.

NO. 6: DARN, PATCH, TURN SHEETS SIDE TO MIDDLE

Obviously. Everyone knows that. But Antigona is forgetting it as hard as she can. My mum catches us binning the toddler's soiled pants: I couldn't do that, she says, because I grew up in the War. Antigona grew up in the War, too, I say. That's why she does it.

NO. 7: KNIT

Knitting is getting trendy, I point out to Antigona. Alternative websites, pieces in the *Guardian*. Maybe we should take it up. Antigona laughs. Her mother, she says, is a genius knitter, can copy any pattern just from seeing it once. So is Jehona. Jehona could sew, too. She would see a dress in a picture, on the TV, then make it, out of the curtains. Perfect. Antigona herself does not knit. 'I can do it, socks and things, but it drive me mad,' she says. 'No you? So boring!' She nearly spits. I remember school knitting lessons, a failed gonk. She's right. Knitting made me feel actually ill. Come the handcrafts revolution, Antigona and I are first up against the wall.

NO. 8: HAND-KNOT RUGS

Thick, gabbeh-style ones rather than the thin, fine sort which cost the eyesight of Kashmiri children. Antigona even says she recognizes the pattern of a very simple rug I bought years ago in Kurdistan: I don't know whether this is an example of Turkish culture living on in Kosovo centuries after the Ottomans left, or whether there are only a limited number of options if you have four colours and a loom. Rug-making does not seem to carry a great deal of cultural baggage for Antigona, though – she says that girls don't make them for dowries or for fertility or specifically for funerals, as they do in different parts of Turkey. Just to keep the floor warm.

I like to think of rugs as being works of art, as creations which give satisfaction to the maker, but Antigona despises the task, because of course it takes hours and hours, and do I know how it leaves your hands? Scarred, and stinking of lanolin. Her sisters, she concedes, felt differently. Vera even seemed to like it. But Vera was always the most patient of the sisters, not vigorous and angry like Blerta, nor wayward and dreamy like Jehona – she was . . . she was . . . 'Meek?' I suggest. 'Gets on my nerves,' says Antigona, knocking her broom thoughtfully on the floor. 'She just stands there and lets them.' When Vera had three small children, she lived in one room with one bed. This bed was decked with rugs to make a dice couch, and her husband sat there every night with his friends, playing till two or three in the morning. The children slept on the floor. Vera stood by the couch, in case one of the men were to want a cup of coffee.

Antigona always talks of her sisters in the present tense, though by the time we have this conversation, it is four years since she has heard from them. She knows for certain that Vera's village went up in smoke. It is well documented. On the TV. Antigona's eyes glass over a moment and her jaw tightens. She goes on beating rugs. Vera could weave, too, she says, and boil wool to make felt – very warm. She made a cradle cover for Flora when she was born, and gloves always, for the winter.

I wonder how many rugs made by how many daughters went up in the fires of the Kosovan wars, how many home-felted cradle covers, how many traditional embroidered skirts and yards of hand-plaited braid, how many cradles and dowry chests handmade from mountain chestnut? I didn't see any on the news pictures, aboard the tractors and donkeys; but there were some in every house, says Antigona, and the dealers of Knightsbridge and Amsterdam had not yet arrived in Kosovo. The refugees, as I remember it, were wrapped in thin, machine-made acrylic blankets, in nylon trousers, in pathetic, smart, Western-style jackets.

NO. 9: CURE CONJUNCTIVITIS

With breast milk. It works. My doctor backs her up. Full of antibiotics, she says.

NO. 10: PREVENT COLDS AND ALLERGIES IN BABIES

Put them to sleep in the byre, or have them strapped to you while you take the cattle out or do the milking. Again, she is right. Early close contact with domestic animals has recently been proved to stimulate children's immune systems.

NO. 11: ELIMINATION TRAINING

Antigona didn't have disposable nappies, or towelling nappies, or a washing machine for her children: she had rags, and plastic bags. So, like all the women she knew, she trained her babies to use the latrine or a basin by holding them over it regularly and making a special chirruping noise until the pee came out. Over time, the chirrup and the holding produce the pee. The process has to be repeated very often and is hugely hard work, but, compared with constantly boiling rags over wood you have personally collected, it represents a saving of labour. Elimination training needs to be done between six weeks and six months, says Antigona, or it will not work, and all the children she knew were continent at one year. Once they can walk, they take themselves to the latrine; before that, they signal to their mother. This is how three-quarters of the world's babies are trained, which is a good thing, for 'disposable' nappies do not biodegrade, and take a great deal of arable land to produce. When Chinese babies move from their current arrangement of trousers with holes to Pampers, the global economy will cease and the world will be covered with landfill. When Antigona mentions her methods at toddler group, though, the ladies say that they would not like to 'psychologically damage' their children by trying such a thing. Some of their four-year-olds are still in nappies, and have, presumably, especially unblemished psyches.

NO. 12: RE-USE, RECYCLE

But properly, under the pressure of absolute poverty. So that a glass bottle has ten years of useful life, so that a plastic bag is reused until its fabric dissolves, so that wedding sheets end their working lives thirty years later as sanitary towels. In reaction to this, 'new' is Antigona's highest term of approbation, as 'authentic' is mine. She usually says it twice, eyes to the sky. When she gets her house, she says – in fact, Antigona spends all her years here on the Council housing waiting list – she will have all appliances in it, new. She will have polished floors, new, new; she will lay them herself. She will have a leather sofa, new, new; she will have a fountain in the front garden, and a marble pond with fish.

She has collected some items already for this house. Velvet curtains from the Debenhams sale. Matching bedclothes in violet. Lacy top sheets. She plans on a dining suite and glassed corner cupboard. She will stack it with china ornaments, especially those with images of children and battery-powered water features. During a family truce, Antigona bought her sister-in-law a family of porcelain rabbits from Argos. The baby rabbit was, she said, the spit of Era's baby clinging endearingly to her mother's coat. Everyone wept on the production of this gift, apparently. But it is not just about subject matter: Antigona has no time for my father-in-law's sentimental Staffordshire pottery, though it often depicts mothers – so faded, so lacking in hyper-real paint and shine. She is enthralled by the sheen of machines: I look for the mark of hand-tools.

Is it just about money? To me, Antigona's luscious ornaments look cheap. But she thinks my nomad's rug, woven circa 1950 in the Caucasus, with its delightful irregularities where the loom was too narrow and its wide-spaced tufts, each dyed in a different diffuse shade of vegetable, makes me look cheap, because within her lifetime she has known people who made and used such items, and they were poor. And she thinks our ripped Thirties leather armchairs are a disgrace, rather than 'vintage'. How long does it take for taste to make the full circle, I wonder, for people to start to admire the otherness of age, rather than the otherness of money? Two generations? Three?

A shorter time. Antigona picks up on her surroundings. She treasures an antique standard lamp I gave her, for instance, though mostly because it is a gilt one. And she admits that her new leather sofas are uncomfortable and a really horrible shade of yellow. She bought them in passion during a row with her brother because Era rang up and said she'd got some. (Of course, they were much marked down.) So they are hate-sofas, and stand opposite each other with the plastic still on them and a lot of space between them, as if one were waiting for the other to ask for a dance.

I stayed in a house in Greenwich once which was ornamented with old agricultural implements: scythes, milking stools, hoes, all the tools Antigona used daily in her former life. There is a shop in Spitalfields called 'field and hand' (lower case, sage on limewash), which sells stripy aprons, cracked enamelware and trowels, for a fortune, only on Sundays. Antigona affects me: I no longer covet these items. They are beautiful, but they look like work. And I think she has a point about the leather armchairs.

NO. 13: TRAP AND ROAST SONGBIRDS

Winter, and we are sugared with snow. A robin comes for bread I've put out.

'Look,' I say to the baby, 'birdie. See the pretty birdie?'

'What is he called?' says Antigona.

'A robin. Do you have those in Kosovo?'

'Yeah. We eat them.'

'Eat them?'

'Yeah. We get a big spoon – wooden spoon you pull bread out of the oven with?'

'Like a spatula?'

'Yeah. And you stand it up so, with a net, and you put food, and sticky stuff for his feet.'

'Lime?'

'And then he comes up and eats, and bang, you catch him.'

'But he's so small. There can't be much eating on a robin.'

'You get lots. Lots of robin. You cover him with – mud? Sticky mud?'

'Clay?'

'Clay. And cook him in the fire. Like lollies. Very yummy.'

'You mean to say you look at a little robin, at a Christmas card, and think, yummy, yummy?'

'No!'

We are laughing helplessly at each other.

'He is gorgeous. He is beautiful. But in the winter we are very hungry.'

NO. 14: FISH

My friend Jeannie has come round, enthused by a book she's just read about the joys of fishing. I remember my grandfather fly-fishing on the Tweed. Neither of us have ever cast a line, or a rod, or whatever it is, but Jeannie thinks we should.

'Did you fish, Antigona?' we ask.

'No,' she says. 'Not sit there hours and hours. We just put a stick of dynamite in. Bang.'

'Then you pick them up in a net?'

'No. Put them in your trousers, jumper. Run away.'

There is that light in her eye. We are certainly being sent up.

NO. 15: KILL THINGS

Chickens, by wringing the neck. Sheep, by slitting the jugular. Rats and mice, by beating with sticks. The last is the only one she will do here. 'I hate it,' she says. 'Killing things. I hate it, every time.'

NO. 16: MILK COWS AND GOATS

Antigona is always threatening to jump over the fence at the community farm and get a cup of warm cow's milk for Sam. Goats, though, she disapproves of. The fleas.

NO. 17: HAGGLE

I find this excruciating, impossible. If someone even asks me if they can help in a shop, I run away.

Antigona, though, is full of fight. She finds it a deprivation, I think, that you cannot bargain in super-stores, and takes revenge by compiling long lists in her head of higher prices which she could have paid but didn't, and then recites them to me. This trait makes her an easy mark for the perpetual 'sales' in places such as JJB Sports, as I have given up trying to explain to her.

I make Antigona come to the farmers' market. She is pleased with some of the produce: 'Fresh,' she says, popping peas, and 'fresh', with 'clean' and 'new', is one of her three sacred terms of approbation. But she is affronted by the prices and appalled that you cannot bargain. She tells the Green Sloane behind the goats' cheese stand that his prices are three times those in Tesco, and he shrugs and will not speak to her, will not even make eye-contact. 'Like I was stupid,' she says, and it is true: he thought she knew nothing, yet she had his business in her bones.

NO. 18: HARROW, PLANT, HOE, TEND, FEED, HARVEST, STORE, START AGAIN

When it comes to the keywords of the green foodie movement – 'seasonal', 'local', and 'organic' – Antigona has walked the walk. For thirty-five years, the only food she tasted that had not been grown within a mile of her door was coffee: Turkish coffee expensively imported and much treasured, which went with white sugar kept exclusively for the purpose. Oh, and Coca-Cola, which was offered only to guests and only as a token of the most extreme munificence. Though fresh grape juice and cold spring water are much nicer, as Antigona freely admits. Everything else was either grown on narrow terraces chipped into the mountain-side (plots often too dry and high for olives and vines, but yielding apricots, plums and seasonal greens, and also supporting chickens and the odd goat), gathered from the hills (chestnuts, mushrooms, berries, song-birds, as above), or, overwhelmingly, milked or slaughtered from the sheep and cows which are the mainstay of the Malësi.

Antigona's memories of food and farming all connect to her mother, who was clearly a skilled manager with an affinity for animals. She knew each cow by name; she called them in and milked them herself; their calves always lived and were heifers much more often than the average. Her mother churned butter by hand, and boiled great pans of milk with vinegar and strained it through muslin to make cheese. Her produce was the best anywhere, everyone said so. Antigona is especially nostalgic for her fresh, unpasteurized butter, and for moons of new cheese, sliced with oil or fried in more butter. When Antigona was married and hungry, her mother made long journeys to bring basketfuls of butter for the children. Antigona had no cow herself then; she was truly dirt poor, and the smallholding where she grew up seemed lush and rich.

The words for 'cow' and 'cheese', too, are literally Antigona's mother tongue. The unique words in Albanian – those untouched by Greek, Latin, Turkish, or Serbo-Croat – are about herding, plants, pasture, animals, milk. The people of the Malësi have been leading a pastoral life, in the literal rather than the literary sense, since there were wooded mountains in Attica and Theocritus was praising them. Even in the twelfth and thirteenth centuries, when the Serbs dominated and cultivated the plain of Kosovo, there were Albanian herdsmen in the mountains, though whether they were driven there or merely allowed to remain is a moot point. Apart from anything else, the mountains, with their acres of bare rocks, their swift streams, their steep narrow valleys and harsh exposed climate – blistering in summer, freezing in winter – will yield no other kind of living.

Pastoral. Antigona still remembers how good it tasted. Lunch on the terrace, under the vine: soft white cheese made fresh that morning, drizzled with bright, peppery cottage olive oil; salad just pulled from the garden, shockingly sweet; flatbread from the oven, tasting of wood smoke. In winter, well-buttered polenta and fatty tasty mutton, stewed till it melted off the bone. Milk-fed lamb at the spring feast, chewed off the ribs like lollipops. Antigona is not to be fooled by bags of salad in Tesco, packets of dyed meat, plastic-wrapped cheese. 'It is shit, actually,' she says.

Though she buys it: nothing gives her greater satisfaction than returning from a super-store with bags and bags of produce. For Antigona remembers the hungry seasons: January to April on polenta and dried beans; no frozen food because the electricity was not reliable; nothing preserved but painstakingly home-bottled tomatoes, some dried beef, mutton stored for weeks in a pit in the ground under sawdust and hay. Food was work: Antigona, like many other Albanian women, got up at four most mornings, and went to bed past midnight. When Antigona was first pregnant, she had nothing to eat but bread and leeks, and her gums went soft and several of her teeth fell out. She remembers what it was to be protein-deprived – to long for meat, and to cook it and serve it to others in the family or to Fazli's interminable guests, and to watch them suck every shred off the bones. She remembers not being able to feed her children. She remembers selling blood to the mobile blood bank in order to buy the children bread, and fainting, over and over again, for days afterwards, because her body could not replenish itself. That blood was sold abroad.

Now when she loads up her kitchen she is immensely proud: she is feeding her family, filling and overfilling what she was brought up to think of as the whole duty of mothers. It is very hard for her to see that different things might be asked of her here: that Mihane, or Mish as she now calls herself, might like her to know which GCSEs she is taking; that the calls from Ylli's school might be fewer if she picked him up herself and talked to his teachers about her problems. When I go round to the maisonette, the girls and Antigona are always in their pyjamas, whatever the time of day. The house is very clean, warm, laundry-smelling. The girls settle beside me on the sofa, giggle about boys – always Albanian boys – who ring them up despite *never* being encouraged to do so. It is the women's quarters; the place where you rest; the place which, in Antigona's experience, makes life tolerable and sustainable; the place you are never allowed to stay in long enough. 'They don't miss anything,' is one of Antigona's constant refrains about her children, and she means heat, comfort and food.

For her first five years here, Antigona works for ten to eighteen hours of every day. She is insistent that each afternoon the girls collect Ylli from school and come straight home to cook, clean and study all evening. I am not so sure. By 2003, when the girls are turning into teenagers, bits of information leak through which point to distress and chaos. Antigona has slapped Mihane because her room is untidy 'like an English girl's'. She has slapped Flora because she will not study, not even one hour a night. The girls don't cook from scratch, Antigona reports with disgust, though they know how to do so. They go through a double pack of kitchen roll every night because they are revolted by tea towels. They let her bags of vegetables rot. They prefer frozen pizza.

6

The Mountain Woman, the Pasha's Wife, and the Problem

Of the strength of the mountain women he boasted greatly. Any one of them, he declared, could start from here with a heavy load of wood to sell in the Bazaar of Scutari, be delivered of a child without any help by the wayside, take child and wood to the bazaar, sell the wood, make purchases, and return home all right.

Someone told the tale of a Pasha of Scutari. Having met upon the road a heavily laden woman carrying the child she had just borne, he questioned her, and at once returned to his wife, who was expecting a child shortly. 'Look here,' said the Pasha, 'I know all about it this time; I'll have no more fuss! The mountain women can shift for themselves, and you must too.' His wife, a wise woman, said nothing, but waited till the Pasha had gone out. Then she bade the servant saddle the Pasha's Arab steed with a wooden samar and take it to the mountains to fetch firewood. When the Pasha came home he found his beautiful Arab raw-backed, broken-kneed, and exhausted. Furious, he asked his wife how she had dared treat it so.

'My dear lord,' she replied, 'you said I must do as the mountain women, so I thought of course your horse could do as the mountain horses.'

From *High Albania*, as told to Edith Durham, 1908

I never intended to become the Pasha's wife.

When I was a child my favourite reading was Victorian girls' stories: *A Little Princess, The Secret Garden, What Katy Did, Little Women*. I loved the exotic landscape of poverty and riches, the eroticized contrasts the narratives so often returned to: the warm houses, luscious dresses and heavy slices of cake of the rich; the crusts, rags, and chill shop doorways of the poor. I understood this to be the past, a past as firmly gone as the troops of slaves and baskets of jewels of my almost equally loved *Arabian Nights*. In the future, I was not to have my own carriage or (blushing, delighted) lady's maid, any more than I was to be the owner of an Arab steed or a gold dress so finely woven it could be drawn through the ring of my little finger. These things existed in a foreign landscape, a place where there were beggars on the street. No one, my mother firmly said, would now countenance such things: people were more equal now, more equal than they'd ever been. Look – the school history book, the illustrated pages turning ever lighter, from the deep purple of the Dark Ages to the light yellow of the Edwardian Era. The Peasants Revolt. The Glorious Revolution. Repeal of the Corn Laws. Sewerage. The Vote. National Insurance. Women's Suffrage. NHS.

They were entwined, these two things, women's freedom and social equality. If I fought for one, I would be fighting for the other. As I grew older, *The Mill on the Floss* and *Jane Eyre* replaced my beloved Hodgson Burnetts. I understood them at once to be about girls seeking a place in the world, and, involved as I was with the injustices meted out to Maggie and Jane, I also took it for granted that my place was to be bigger than theirs, and that it was to be given me as a right. No one would tell me I could not learn Latin, or that girls were 'quick and shallow'. No one would stop me going to school. Jane, Maggie, Katy, Laura of the Ingalls Wilder books, even Jo of *Little Women*: all might be broken by poverty or accidents or seduced by sleigh rides or distant lieutenants into corsets and frilled frocks and housework, but not me. I and all girls like me were to have jobs.

We did. In the UK, women of my generation, born in the 1960s and 1970s, are the first to form a significant minority and even sometimes a majority in education, medicine, law and journalism. Through the Thatcher years, the 1980s and 1990s, we laboured alongside our brothers, fought for similar salaries, and helped to create the longest professional working hours in Europe. O Brave New World, as Antigona does indeed see it. But not for her: because a lot of that liberated female energy went into making private money rather than changing the world. The 1970s turned out to be a high-water mark of family income parity, not a staging post on the way to Utopia. Since then, the gap between the richest and the poorest in our society has much increased, and social mobility, instead of becoming absolute, has stalled.

All through the 1980s and 1990s in Britain, and unbridled into the twenty-first century, taxes on the top level of income tax went down and the highest salaries went up. Professional women were able to use these higher earnings to buy flats or to form dual-earner partnerships and buy houses, and thus to underwrite the vast rise in house prices. Housing accounts for the majority of private wealth in Britain, and its value rose exponentially from the mid 1990s onwards, until the middle-class owners of modest Victorian terraces found they possessed hundreds of thousands of pounds. I bought a flat in Spitalfields in 1992, easily, on a teacher's salary; by the time I met Antigona in 2001, rises in its value and a move up the property ladder meant that I, who have never earned more than £20,000 a year, had 200 times as much capital as she; a gap she had no hope of closing.

The same decade had also brought me quantities of consumer goods, for those were the years of globalization. When I was reading *The Arabian Nights* I owned a single Marks & Spencer sweater for out-of-school-wear, 100% wool, made in Yorkshire. Now I may not have a golden robe, but I have twenty sweaters, made in China. I am not served by a thousand barefoot Nubian slaves (the *Arabian Nights* are startlingly racist), but music is played to me and many chores are done by machines made by people of whose lives I have only the shadiest concept. The story of Aladdin has a problem with realizing the hero's ever-increasing wealth: it keeps having to add extra, identical, palaces and absurdly large jewels to the tally of Aladdin's goods in order to extend a desire which seemed at first fulfilled by a good meal on a good plate. This is where I am in 2001, when I meet Antigona: I have everything I want; I have to strain to think of a birthday gift; I wear clothes 'ironically'; I search out battered armchairs. Antigona comes from a country which has not even begun capitalism, which has nothing but state-run quarries and wrecked collective farms, which has recently been devastated by war. The day I meet her, her possessions would fit into a suitcase.

Ylli is pressing his balloon into Sam's hand, squeezing the baby's fingers carefully round the string. He is starting his education in an era when the likelihood of his rising up the British social ladder and Sam sinking down it is slimmer than in the 1950s. Above Sam, too, there is a new, growing, class of plutocrats, City workers as many times richer than Antigona as ever Victorian gentlemen were than their maids. A few of them are women, and somehow, that does not feel like a victory.

Antigona and I look at each other. We are both handsome, outspoken women; we had both been hopeful, defiant girls, but now, despite ourselves, we are the Mountain Woman and the Pasha's Wife, and because we share a certain shrewd intuition, we know it.

'Do you want a job?' I ask.

This is the job I want Antigona to do:

In a small three-bedroom house (Victorian two-up two-down, extension out the back, attic conversion; you know the one), the sweeping, the vacuuming, the mopping, the dusting, the waxing of the ground floor; the dragging out of bin bags, the washing of the bin, the cleaning of the kitchen sink, the scrubbing of the kitchen surfaces, the chipping of Weetabix from the baby's high chair, the gathering up of the baby's toys and the cleaning of them; the sorting of laundry, the placing it in the machine, the hanging of it, the ironing, the re-sorting of it and the replacing of it in drawers; the carrying of the vacuum cleaner and the mop upstairs, the cleaning of the bathroom, the bedrooms, the study, the mopping of the stairs and bathroom floor; the carrying of the vacuum cleaner and the mop downstairs and the ramming of the vacuum in the cupboard and the placing of the mop upside down, outside to dry.

I don't suppose you read that sentence. No one wants to talk about the housework. When I was planning my glorious career, when my contemporaries were planning theirs, we did not give it a second thought. It baffles me now, when I think about it. Who did I think was going to do it? What did I think my mother did all day until I was five, which was when, scandalously early in those days, she went back to work? Did I think housework would be abolished, because we had vacuum cleaners, in the same way that antibiotics seemed to herald the end of illness? What kind of scorn must I have had for women when I planned to do only men's work?

It's like the baby. I used to think they were making it up, those women who didn't come back to the staffroom after their first child. What could they be doing all day? But my own baby has taken every scrap of my energy, every minute of my time. Sam is ten months old when I meet Antigona, and I've started sending him to nursery every morning for three hours. I need to spend those three hours writing: in order to pay for the nursery, apart from anything else. I tend to spend them on the stairs, though, between a pile of washing and an old copy of the *TLS*, unable to decide whether to carry it upstairs or mop the floor. Something has to be done.

The beloved books of my youth were a lot about housework, now I come to see them clearly, about learning to do it: to clean a house, the work of it; to make a garden, the work of it; these are the journeys of the Little Princess and Frances Hodgson Burnett's other famous heroine, Mary Lennox. Laura Ingalls learns to come in from her prairie and sew; Katy Did get her back literally broken in order to absorb the same lesson. Mrs Tulliver, that poor stupid thing, is calling Maggie in to fold the linen, to help her with the work, the work. I can hear them all clearly now, the mothers' voices, now the work falls to me, now it is me doing the calling.

Eight pounds an hour for the whole boiling, is what I first offer Antigona. All Antigona's children come round with her to inspect the property, and I clean up massively first.

'My mum says she will do the job,' says Mihane. 'But it's not enough hours. You need to find her more jobs.'

I look at Antigona, over by the bucket. 'Live on one hundred and forty-one pound a week income support?' she says, brandishing the mop, her accent suddenly spot-on Estuary. 'You're kidding me!'

'OK,' I say. 'Yeah. No problem.'

And it isn't. I ring round my friends.

'You need the time if you're going to be seriously freelance,' I say.

And, 'With both of you working, something has to give.'

And, 'It's all very well when you're dinkies, but it's different when you've got a kid.'

And, 'I know he should do more round the house . . . yeah, I know it drives you mad . . . but this could just take the heat out of it and maybe you could start getting on better.'

And, 'Go on. You deserve some time to yourself.'

And, 'It's an investment in your house, really.'

And, 'I know it's against your ideals, but the world's not so ideal.'

And, 'Well, it is kind of feminist. She's divorced, you know. Battered wife.'

And, 'Eight pounds an hour.'

And, 'Yeah. Fantastic. Should see her mopping.'

It takes me just one evening and six phone calls to find Antigona twenty-eight hours of work, and one week and one card in our local newsagents' to find another fourteen, so clearly I'm not alone in my inability to deal with the housework. I don't believe my little area is unique, either – though it is sufficiently stratified by house prices to contain a larger than average number of couples who need two incomes to pay their mortgages and who are also beginning to have young families.

They are very female conversations, my phone calls, confidential and cosy, depending on the mutual confession of weaknesses, giggling, trust. As if I were selling moustache removers or vibrators, as if I were the Avon Lady or the Ann Summers rep. Or as if I were

Betty Friedan in 1959, when she heard *'a mother of four, having coffee with four other mothers in a suburban development fifteen miles from New York, say in a tone of quiet desperation, "the problem". And the others knew, without words, that she was not talking about a problem with her husband, or her children, or her home. Suddenly they realized they all shared the same problem, the problem that has no name. They began, hesitantly, to talk about it. Later, after they had picked up their children at nursery school and taken them home to nap, two of the women cried, in sheer relief, just to know they were not alone.'*

The 'problem' in 1959 was women's shame over their wish to work outside the home, whereas ours in 2001 was shame at our inability to work outside the home or even inside the home without the home collapsing. One of my woman friends weeps on the phone after Antigona's first visit, so relieved is she by the mopped-ness, the sudden fresh tidiness of her home. 'I just don't feel bad any more,' she says. Others describe similar epiphanies as we stand round the swings in the playground. 'It is because we feel responsible for our houses,' says one. 'Personally responsible. So guilty.' As if they were our bodies. As if we had been brought up under the Kanun of Lck. Our 'problcm' may vcry wcll bc with be with our husbands, too, because, when we have children, we suddenly find ourselves, as Naomi Wolf brilliantly described in *Misconceptions,* unequal to them, doing lower-status work, and this can breed all kinds of resentment.

How can we have come so far and yet still be

weeping with shame in the scullery? Friedan intended housework to become a public issue. *The Feminine Mystique* smokes with rage about housework and being brainwashed into doing it. It was the cause célèbre of the Women's Movement in the 1960s. 'Wages for Housework' was a serious slogan, not a joke, in the 1970s. I and my contemporaries were supposed to be the beneficiaries of all that. Somewhere along the line, somewhere when we were donning our power suits and tutting about a woman in the office who kept leaving at five to see her children, we forgot its importance.

We have developed no proper, serious way of talking about housework in this country. The work of wives in the home is acknowledged (to red-top derision) in divorce settlements and (barely) in pensions, but does not figure in any other public discourse, unlike, for example, childcare. Surveys on the balance of work within the home consistently show that women carry the burden, but such surveys remain small scale and sociological, because housework does not have economic consequences: whether or not the floor is clean has only tiny, incremental effects on public health. Nor do we have proper figures or statistics about cleaning. Estimates of the numbers of private cleaners in this country vary between two and three million, but they can never be more than estimates, because most private cleaning is done privately, untaxed and unregistered, as indeed I start out with Antigona, or by completely unregistered 'invisible' immigrants.

Women collude in this: we accept that the house is our responsibility and our shame, whether or not we are working the same hours as our male partners. We solve the problem by buying takeaways or by taking on an invisible, untaxed person to help us, rather than by quarrelling fruitlessly with our partners or by making what would doubtless be seen as an outlandish and ludicrous fuss with our employers.

So we ignore it – until we have children. Children, for professional women, tend to be spoken of as an expense, a dream, a difficulty, a thing, like 'commitment', never to be mentioned to men. When both partners in a couple are working in professional jobs modelled to fit men with wives, jobs whose hours have increased, not decreased, since the 1970s, it is difficult to see where to *fit children in*. Like the house, children are often regarded as something women want, an indulgence or a hobby, which they must therefore pay for. Difficult decisions tend to be put off: a quarter of women born, like me, in 1965 reached forty without children, and that has never happened before in our history. Almost all professional mothers had children later than ever before, in our mid to late thirties, and found, like me, that they left us tired. We returned to workplaces whose harsh hours we had helped create and found that it was more politic to excuse absence by saying our cars had broken down than that our children were ill. The career gap and the stress of childbearing ensured that male majorities at the very top weren't rocked. Some of us, like me, went part-time or freelance, or gave up altogether, and found ourselves back in the house, confronting the work of it: mothers, wives.

And then we have to do the housework, and there is much more housework to do. We find we have made our own beds, and not especially well, because we hadn't paid adequate attention to bed-making in the first place. We have eschewed a public solution to bed-making because we thought we didn't need one, and now we have a big private Problem. What to do but phone each other up about refugees who are good at mopping? And, sometimes, to worry about whether this is feminism or not.

These are the jobs Antigona ends up doing:

Monday: Three hours' cleaning for the illustrator. Four hours' cleaning for the lawyer.

Tuesday: Two hours' cleaning for the acupuncturist. (Nice job, as it is all very clean and oily-smelling to start with.) Four hours' cleaning for the publisher. (Nasty job. Too many children, too few hours.)

Wednesday: Four hours' cleaning for me. Three hours' cleaning for Jeannie (we are both messy, but are forgiven as we count as friends).

Thursday: Three hours' cleaning for an old lady. (Worthy job, as old lady clearly cannot clean for herself.) Four hours' cleaning for rich lady with no job. (Antigona hates her. The lady hangs around and makes suggestions as to how she should clean.)

Friday: Four hours' cleaning for Jeannie. (Jeannie is unique in not underestimating the amount of help she needs, making her an A* employer.) Four hours cleaning for the academic (very tidy, very much in contrast with me).

In addition, Antigona works at waitressing every weekend and some evenings. She starts off in outside catering, weddings and parties, then moves on to a conference centre and learns silver service. She likes it, she says. At a function at a literary festival, she meets Bill Clinton, and despite her name badge identifying her as an Italian called Anna, succeeds in thanking him for her life and for the lives of the people of Kosovo. He was pleased, apparently; but Hillary wasn't.

So the illustrator, the lawyer, the acupuncturist, the old lady's busy daughter, Jeannie, and I, all get a better Life Work Balance after Antigona comes to work for them. We get more Quality Time with our children. We get more Couple Time with our spouses. Antigona, on the other hand, doesn't. She takes on more and more work. Not content with cleaning for forty hours a week, she starts work in an Italian restaurant for a further six evenings. She works late, till at least midnight. Most days, she only comes home between five and six in the evening, during which time she cooks, showers and changes into her uniform.

The third house she lives in while on the Council housing waiting list, the one she stays in for three years, is in a block half a mile away from me. It's a maisonette – warm, clean, and cosy but very small. The girls share a room with just space for their beds and wardrobe, Ylli has a 5 ft by 6 ft boxroom. There are no books in this house, no desks, no files. The television is on constantly. Sam's advantage over Ylli is not just space and money; it is time. I use some of the time Antigona saves for me on Sam: reading to him, playing with him, practising deferred gratification. Antigona, who is as vivid a talker as anyone, who is an education to be with, does not have that time for Ylli. He stays up too late watching TV. He gets into trouble at school.

I become concerned for Flora, too, who achieved so highly in her first two years here. When she goes into the sixth form, she seems to lapse: Antigona reports huge attacks of teenage apathy, quarrels with Mihane, days when Flora clearly has not gone to school. I offer to tutor her in English A level, but Flora is a difficult pupil. Not in her manner – her manner is excellent: the dimpled, smiley keenness best calculated to appease a teacher, to get them telling amusing stories of their home life or what they did in the War. Nor is she in the least unintelligent, or illiterate. She reads certain books I give her with great appetite: *The Bookseller of Kabul*, *My Antonia*. But her spelling and handwriting are poor, her point of view often bizarre – you cannot get a pass mark, Flora, if you spend most of the essay speculating on whether or not the poet is a virgin – and she seems profoundly distracted. She comes round to use my computer but prints nothing out. I check the history of my internet browser and find it full of horoscope sites and Albanian chatrooms. She lands Antigona with a £396 phone bill by calling mediums on premium-rate phone lines, and it takes all my negotiating skills to persuade BT not to cut them off. I lend her *I Capture the Castle* and she doesn't turn up any more.

HOW GERMAINE GREER (IN 1970) WOULD SOLVE 'THE PROBLEM'

Brilliant women are not reproducing themselves because childbearing has been regarded as a full-time job; genetically they might be thought to be being bred out. In a situation where a woman might contribute a child to a household which engages her attention for part of the time while leaving her free to frequent other spheres of influence, brilliant women might be more inclined to reproduce. For some time now I have pondered the problem of having a child which would not incur the difficulties I would have in adjusting to a husband and the demands of domesticity. A plan, by no means a blueprint, evolved which has become a sort of dream . . . I thought again of the children I knew in Calabria and hit upon the plan to buy, with the help of some friends with similar problems, a farmhouse in Italy where we could stay when circumstances permitted, and where our children would be born. Their fathers and others would also visit the house as often as they could, to rest and enjoy the children and even work a bit. Perhaps some of us would live there for quite long periods, as long as we wanted to. The house and garden would be worked by a local family who lived in the house.'

(Germaine Greer, *The Female Eunuch*, 1970)

A family from Calabria in the 1970s would be excellent. The mopping would surely be outstanding, to say nothing of the cooking and gardening. Nothing like subsistence farming in extreme but tastefully Mediterranean poverty to hone those vital household skills.

As, of course, I have found with Antigona. By employing her and paying her everything I earn through writing, I am able to enjoy mothering part-time and am also able to carry on being 'a brilliant woman' who 'frequents other spheres'. So, in different ways and ratios, are Jeannie, the illustrator, the lawyer, the academic, and the publisher. So, in one way, Greer is simply correct. But Greer's 'local family' didn't get to have 'other spheres'. I don't see how one woman's 'brilliance' depending on another woman's immersion in household labour can possibly be a long-term or ethical solution to Greer's – and my – Problem.

The more time I spend with Antigona, the more I think she is a 'brilliant woman': outstandingly quick, verbal, sympathetic, ingenious, satirical, strong-minded, resilient and original. She has ended up working for me purely because of her minimal formal education and her very rich and thorough and highly enforced training in household and agricultural skills. Her whole body has been shaped to labour: she squats to clean with that deep strong motion Western women learn only in yoga classes, though when I see her running and catching balls and playing keepy-uppy with the children, I can tell she has the sort of innate athletic ability which makes a professional tennis player or PE teacher, at the least. And her mind has been limited: she speaks three languages beautifully but has never read a book. She can do vast comparative sums in her head but cannot calculate a percentage on paper. She is extremely shrewd and intuitive, and deeply, saltily cynical, but she has had no education in abstract concepts: she grew up under communism but has no idea what the term means. She has left the village behind, but keeps bumping up against it in her mind, against the shadow of the Kanun, against Shame.

I like to think of housework and child-work as being creative. In my life, that is how they function: a rich, earthy, anchoring force. But in Antigona's life, an education in housework has removed the possibility of being creative. Antigona didn't want to weave or spin: she wanted to talk and learn, and she missed her chance. Much as she has changed here, the change from the life of the body to the life of the pen is beyond her. This exceptionally verbal woman will never write because she was forced to clean instead of reading; this gifted linguist will never translate; this swift athlete will never know how high she could have jumped, and I benefit by her stunting.

Greer is surely right to say that the family must be more flexible and that mothers must be able to do things other than mother – it's just that 'mothers' must include Antigona. 'Brilliant women' are in no danger of being 'bred out': rather, they are everywhere suppressed. We cannot create an ideal family set-up in Calabria, nor in any other South, off the backs of women who have had other possibilities in their lives removed. We need to change ourselves and we need to change the way we live and the place we live. We have to change the nature of a job – every job, men's and women's – from something which is designed to be done by someone who is cared for at home in every practical way to something designed to be done by someone who also has responsibility for practical caring. Everyone, male and female, needs to spend substantially less time in the workplace and substantially more time caring for children, ourselves and our homes. If we want to be feminists, if we want women to be free, all women, then we need to live differently here.

7

Nannies, Maids, and *The Revenger's Tragedy*

Hi There,

I am looking for a Nanny/Housekeeper (LIVE IN) in a wonderful loving home in Berkshire.

Duties: The main job here is caring for my 5 month old son, feeding, bathing and generally playing and walking him. My son is very loving but very playful so we need someone who loves to play with children and can still keep an eye out for things that need to be done in the house.

I work 4 nights a week and therefore you will have to do the night feeds (about 2 a night).

I usually get home between 3–4 am in the morning so I will need to sleep till 1–2 pm.

The other duties are keeping the house very clean, Ironing and changing bed sheets weekly, making a light breakfast & some dinner and very little gardening like watering plants. Generally we need someone who is loving and caring to look after us. This job is not just about the money, Its [sic] about being part of the family. We will take care of you and love you and expect the same back.

We will need references, Police checks and CV's and I would prefer if you wore a nanny/housekeeper uniform.

We will pay £600 a month and one day off a week and a paid holiday for two weeks once you have been with us at least 12 months.

Advertisement on London Gumtree, July 2007.
One of many

'The Maids' is the name of our local cleaning service. I often see their vans parked in nearby streets, jauntily emblazoned with a saucy round-bottomed lady in a lace apron. Ironic, of course – no one says 'maid'. The pallid, heavy-footed gangs of women I occasionally see dragging mops from the van or smoking in the front seats wear badges which say 'cleaning operative'. Their pay is shit, says Antigona. They are low-grade women, stupid. Polish. Imagine, says Antigona, if you had your EU papers and you still needed to work in a job like that. Ha. She tosses her black ponytail.

I think of the salary list of an Edwardian grand house: handwritten in cursive, arranged by hierarchies: scullery maid, under-kitchen maid, kitchen-maid, under-cook, cook; bootboy, under-footman, footman, butler; skivvy, housemaid, housekeeper; the upper servants and the lower, the body servants – lady's maid, valet; the between-stairs people – governess, companion. We visit great houses to be horrified by these now: the ranked bells, the attic bedrooms, the back stairs – but at least they acknowledge the scale of the task of housekeeping, and the differentiation of skills. In terms of raw numbers, if not of proportion, we probably have more servants now in Britain than we did at the turn of the century, but their jobs are not differentiated – cleaner, cleaning operative, housekeeper – and their proper names are very often not recorded. When people have no rank, not even a lowly rank, we tend, I think, to treat them worse.

'My mother says "maid",' says my friend Monique. She is from Trinidad. The maid, Diana, has served her mother for twenty-five years. She is twenty years younger than her employer, but now they are both old, just a pair of old ladies gossiping in Creole on the terrace. For twenty-five years, Monique's mother has paid every doctor's visit for Diana and her family, written all letters, made all official phone calls, and built Diana's house. In return, Diana has cared for the house, nursed Monique's grandmother, and now Monique's mother. Actually, says Monique, Diana no longer cleans, but how can you fire someone who laid out your grandmother's body, pulled her twisted ribs into alignment, someone who will, you may be perfectly certain, hold your mother's hand when she dies?

The woman up the road is not allowed to employ Antigona. Her husband forbids it. They get The Maids in instead, once a week for four hours, during which time she is always in the playground so that the children don't witness any of the process. 'It's the personal element,' she says, helplessly. 'I mean, don't you find that difficult? Talking to them? And my husband's worse, he's terrible! He just doesn't want to know, you know, who is cleaning his personal things. Gives him the creeps.' She shrugs, smiles. Men. 'Silly, but then, at the end of the day, it's his money.'

The personal element. The individual. Yes, I should say to my neighbour, it is difficult, it is embarrassing. It makes explicit a relationship which I would rather ignore: the relationship of my freedom to another's labour, my wealth to another's poverty. Maybe it would be easier to pretend it is not happening, easier to employ a firm called 'The Maids' and call them 'cleaning operatives' – machines, not women. In the same way, it suddenly occurs to me, as I found it easier to send Sam to a nursery rather than a childminder. A childminder is an individual, and individuals demand interaction. They make you feel worse.

But Sam was never happy at nursery. He wanted an individual. In 2004, he was due to start state nursery school and I was due to have a new baby. My friend Jeannie, meanwhile, had a seven-month-old baby, two older children, and a new job. Neither of us was able to pretend we could have it all, any more; neither of us wanted to hand another baby into group care; but neither of us wanted to give up our jobs, either. We both knew and employed Antigona, and we knew that 'Nanny' was a title she fancied more than 'cleaning operative', and so we had our obvious but brilliant idea. Together, we reckoned, by paying her most of my earnings and about half of what Jeannie takes home, we could employ Antigona five days a week and pay her £16,000 a year, which, from our reading of Working Tax Credit regulations (we have both received it) should still entitle Antigona to some support and, more crucially, to Housing Benefit. In return, Antigona would solve the Problem for us. Antigona could work in my house in the morning, taking care of the babies and picking up the little ones from nursery school, and at three o'clock could move to Jeannie, collecting Ylli from school on the way alongside Jeannie's son. It would help Ylli. Antigona could do an NVQ in childcare! We were excited by our benign, liberal plan. We couldn't wait to tell Antigona.

Except that she will have none of it. It's not the childcare – she wants to do that. It's the taxes. She refuses, point-blank, to go legal. She will end up paying tax, she will not have enough money. I realize, with a crunch, that going legal was what the owner of the sweet factory wanted her to do. Rather than take her passport, he was trying to rid her of the man taking her wages and filling her with fear about the tax system. Now, Antigona says, she knows no one who pays tax. But she already pays tax, we point out, for the restaurant. Maximum tax, actually, in the name of Anna Grimaldi, an imaginary Italian. If she was legal, she could get that back. Antigona says she could not possibly declare that much income, because then she would lose her Housing Benefit, which is more than a thousand pounds a month. We say that if she starts paying National Insurance she will be entitled to a pension. She looks at us as if we were cretins.

Also, we say, it is one thing for each of us to employ her four hours a week and pay cash. That's not even illegal. But employing her full-time without tax is different. We would be committing a crime. Antigona says no one is ever caught for this crime. We say they are. Who do we know? asks Antigona. We say no one – but we've read about them. Antigona thinks nothing of such evidence. Antigona says we know nothing of the real world, by which she means the black economy. We say we've read about it. Ten per cent of GDP, isn't it? There, says Antigona. You see. One in ten, and how many get caught? Maybe one in 10,000. Impasse.

Jeannie and I start to ask ourselves: How Much is Antigona Earning, 2002–3?

And we add it up: A Large Sum:

Income Support and Child Benefit: £135
Cleaning 30–40 hours a week, £8 an hour: £250
Restaurant 30 hours a week, £4.50 an hour, minus tax and NICs: £100
Restaurant tips, approx. £20 a night: £100
Average weekly income = £585

But Antigona also receives more than £300 each week in Housing Benefit. She needs this because, though her house was built by the Council, it was bought by its tenant some years ago. A few changes of hands later, it has become a rental property whose high commercial rate has to be met by the Council because they have a shortage of properties because tenants keep buying them. If Antigona had a council house with a £70 rent, she could, she tells us, afford to pay tax.

Including the Housing Benefit, her weekly income becomes about £500, nearly £50,000 per annum net income. For a tax-paying person to bring home such an income, she would have to earn at least £70,000 gross. So, though my hourly rate can sometimes be a great deal higher than Antigona's, and though I have a house which through no virtue or talent or mine accumulates yearly more than Antigona can earn, I am a long way from being able to employ her. My gross income varies between £10,000 and £16,000 a year; Jeannie's new job pays £29,000.

I am depressed by my sum. I have never been one for the *Daily Mail*, never believed in a plague of black-market immigrants living it up off benefits. Clearly, Antigona is not living it up. She is glassy-eyed and stick thin and never sleeps. But even allowing for the fact that she never actually sees the Housing Benefit, she must still be saving money. Where, then, is she putting it, I ask her. She is, she says:

1. Still paying back her own and Fazli's passage money (the £13,000 has grown to nearer £20,000) to her brothers so that they will not fall foul of the nefarious figures they bribed in the first place.
2. Saving up to go to Albania to look for her family.
3. Saving up so that she will not be penniless if she is deported. Recently, she has been refused the immigration amnesty granted to many Kosovars by the Home Office, on the grounds, her lawyer reckons, that she is related to a criminal: Fazli. The fact that the majority of his crimes were committed against her is, apparently, irrelevant. The lawyer is not appealing because Antigona has nearly two years left of her Leave to Remain, and so can apply for those papers to be renewed in the ordinary way. Nevertheless, the event has frightened her horribly. Kosovars are now being repatriated, Antigona knows. Kosovo is supposed to be safe. But Antigona herself cannot go back to Kosovo, she says, because Fazli or Fazli's family will kill her. So she needs to save enough money to get herself and her children somewhere else, perhaps Italy, and start life again illegally.

I find it hard to argue with any of this. I also know that it is true she is one of very many. Migrant labour, much of it illegal, sustains our catering and cleaning industries and, if you figure in private cleaning, too, much else. All the working women I know employ a cleaner; Jeannie and I are the only ones wrestling with the extremely complex tax credit system. Even the Home Office, it emerges a couple of years later, is cleaned by illegal migrant labour.

And I know that Antigona is right to say that very few get caught. How can I ever persuade her to come and work for me when she earns so much more than I do? How can I make working for less money an attractive, even a possible idea? Jeannie says we can't. We dig deeper and work out how to pay her more. We get in a third family for some afternoons. We get the exact Housing Benefit figures from the Council. They're on a sliding scale, actually: not so bad. We put this new proposition to her. We wait.

Nothing. I try again.

'Antigona,' I say, 'I think you should pay tax because it's part of belonging to this society. Taxes pay for schools and hospitals and the police, and you like all those things. And it wouldn't be very much tax, and I'll pay it. Really, we can work it out.'

Antigona shoves another load in the washing machine. She won't meet my eye. 'I'm going to Albania,' she says. 'Next week.'

'What? What about the children?'

'Ylli will come with me – the girls will be OK.'

'No, they won't.'

'Flora is seventeen.'

'Still . . . Are you going to look for your family?'

'Yes.'

'How? I mean, where?'

'Tirana – capital city. Then Vlores, in south. There is nice beach there. Then – around.'

'But Antigona. We went through this, remember? The Red Cross? We checked all the lists?' I'm saying her family are dead. Understandably, she is not listening.

'You don't understand. In Albania, they don't have lists.'

This seems plausible.

'So, my job – you will make up your mind when you come back?'

'When I come back.'

The trip is of course a much bigger deal than that. I have to buy the air tickets, which she says are too expensive. I have to lend suitcases, find the bus times. Antigona is calmly adamant about all this, and I start to believe she will make her way coolly through Heathrow, perhaps even track down her family by simply badgering an official until they take down some forgotten ledger and trace their names with an inky thumb.

Of the wisdom of leaving the girls I am less convinced. They have a school term to finish, true, and exams, and Antigona simply believes they will go there every day, and come back and cook in the empty house. She leaves them money. I call them a few times while she is away, and they giggle, but I am heavily pregnant and have my eye off the ball.

Antigona is gone three weeks. When she comes back,

she is tanned from her sojourn in Vlores, but strangely dead round the eyes. She found nothing, though she asked at many agencies, and trekked through three major cities.

She says she will take my job, and we go to the job centre and sign many hundreds of forms. She lends me a tenner on the way out, to buy fruit in the market, and we both laugh our heads off. She is doing it for me, she says. She does not accept anything I have to say about the future, or pensions, or GNVQs, or strengthening her case to remain here. But I am like her sister here, and this what I want. And her real sisters are dead, we have to assume now: Vera, Blerta, Jehona, and their children. Her own mother is dead, we have to assume: Fatmire, who was such a tower of strength to her. When my baby is born, Antigona cries with joy.

This is the deal, then, and it is good to have it explicit. Antigona comes into my family and loves my children as her own. You cannot pay for that, therefore she is part of my family: my sister. I have never had a sister, but seems to me it must be the person you hand the baby to; the person you can spend several hours with and only talk to occasionally, or talk to for half an hour about whether the baby is ready for pureed carrot; the person whose pain you feel viscerally even when you think you disagree with her intellectually; the person you quarrel with in the certain knowledge that you will still have to know her.

None of my plans for Antigona turn out to be any good, though. She would simply have been richer had I allowed her to continue to work illegally. The things

I give her which do help her in her life are the same gifts a Victorian lady might give her maid: my references, my influence, and my posh English accent which she learns to imitate so well over the phone.

Soon after she starts working as a nanny, Antigona meets Era in the market. Not the Islington Farmers' Market, but the rough Goldsmith Row Wednesday market, the one with fruit and sinisterly cheap cheese. She is pushing the babies, mine and Jeannie's. Antigona and Agim are at the time in the middle of a dispute over whether Mihane should take a Saturday job at M&S or whether this is tantamount to prostitution. Era points at the babies: 'Aren't you ashamed,' she says, 'to work like that?'

'No,' says Antigona. 'I am proud of them. Very proud. They are beautiful. They are mine.'

She barges past Era and doesn't cry till she gets home.

THE INSTRUCTIVE STORY OF AUNTIE VITTORIA

This happens a year later, when Antigona is a fully fledged nanny and, as happens most mornings, is proudly rocking my toddler on a swing in the playground while Jeannie's daughter clambers up the climbing frame. Two stranger children are behaving badly – dashing under the swing, pulling on the baby's legs, and running away from their carer, a distracted-looking lady with bleached black hair falling out of a bun. Antigona takes any assault on her baby very seriously, so she collars the children, shouts at them, then, because all children must love her, sorts them out on a swing each. She turns to the lady, intending to deliver a piece of her mind, only to encounter a flood of gratitude and apology in Albanian.

Auntie Vittoria, it emerges over milky coffee at the Drop-In Centre, through whose portals Antigona has now guided her, is a slave. That is, she was brought here by an Italian woman who was once married to Vittoria's husband's cousin. The Italian woman has long since moved on from her Albanian husband and had two children with another man, but, for reasons of mutual convenience, she has never divorced the Albanian. The Italian woman now has a busy management job in some sort of office in the City, and, especially since her children's father left, has a very big Problem. So she got her Albanian nominal husband to invite Vittoria to come here on a guest visa, promising her £1000 for six months' nannying. Vittoria sleeps in the children's room (except nobody sleeps), and is at the kids' beck and call all day long. The children are angry and difficult as they have had many different nannies; and Vittoria speaks no English; and she doesn't get fed regularly; and recently, the mother went away for a week and left Vittoria with only £20 for food for the whole time, and the children didn't go hungry; but she did. And she didn't know the Drop-In was there, and she gazes in wonder at its scratched tables and easy warmth. Antigona buys her a sandwich. She is furious. Vittoria is her mother's age.

'You can't go to the police, though,' I point out.

'She'll be deported.' And, because I can't resist; and really the tax is quite heavy, and I hate the forms: 'See – that's what I pay tax for. So you don't get into that kind of mess.'

Later, when the Italian woman abruptly decides to go back to Italy and pay Vittoria nothing for her five months' slavery, on the grounds that she has not finished her contract, Antigona goes round to the house and tests her knowledge of Neapolitan abuse and the English legal system. She comes back with £500 – enough to send Vittoria home with some credit. Vittoria falls to her knees and kisses Antigona's feet. She says Antigona is an angel, and a very, very clean and virtuous woman despite her lack of a husband. Antigona is highly pleased with the whole adventure.

'You see,' she tells me smugly, 'it is not about tax. It is about if you have a strong head or no.'

Back to 2004. The first weeks with the new baby. Summer, sunlight slanting through the window, the baby asleep, crumpled like washing in her fleece-lined Moses basket, everything shining where Antigona has polished it: the blanket chest, the tiles, my coffee cup full of sweet, milky café latte. We are in the women's quarters, snug and laundry-smelling. I seem to spend a lot of time in the bath.

Antigona has taken to her new job. She loves it. She holds the new baby as if she were her own, chatters and sings to her in Albanian; hands her back to me and turns to feed Jeannie's baby in her high chair, laughing with each spoonful. At three she leaves for Jeannie's, picking up Ylli and the bigger children on the way. Everything should be good, I feel, should settle as the little one is settling, as she learns day by day the way we live here.

But, when I come to focus on her, I see that Antigona is not settled. Not that she doesn't look good: in fact, with her thin, brown body now constantly on display in a range of tight jeans and tighter vest tops, her lush hair bobbed and rinsed purple, and her dark eyes kholed, her appearance is terrific, especially against the light from the other end of the room. Close up, she seems a little odd, wall-eyed and pallid, an anxious twitch around her mouth. She is still working in the restaurant all hours, six to midnight at least. She won't think of giving it up. She is making a lot of money, £30 a night in tips alone.

She loves it, actually. She is wonderfully good at it – can effortlessly memorize a huge order, carry four plates up her arm, smile at the flirty older man and the crying baby. Mr Happy Eater, the restaurant inspector, comes in and awards her 96 per cent, twice, for her performance. Every morning she tells me of compliments received, another toddler charmed, another woman who couldn't believe she was the mother of a teenager, another man begging for her phone number, another idiot bus driver bested on her journey home. It is theatre for her, I think, an arena for her inner, long-repressed performer. The licensed flirting in particular thrills her: after all, she has never had any fun out of what she knows to be her great good looks. Here, in the wine fug, under the dim lights, she can play the young girl, the village beauty.

And it gets her out of the house, where all is not well, either. While Antigona was in Albania, Flora failed to get her AS level in English, and Mihane picked up only four good GCSEs. I think, and the school thinks, that this is pretty good for a girl who has been in the country only since Year 8, and who had a very sketchy primary education, but Antigona's expectations are infinite. Mihane wants to go on to do GNVQ Business at college now, but Antigona is opposed: it should be school, A' levels, and university. I persuade her to let Mihane take the more practical option, and the furore is soon forgotten in a much greater trouble: Flora has a boyfriend.

Of course, Flora has a boyfriend. Really, you should see her. Only Mihane has inherited her mother's sexy figure; neither daughter has that lovely flaring jawline or elegant nose, but Flora at eighteen, with her wide, wide eyes, white skin, and long, curling mouth, has a charm all her own: the charm of a kitten treading its stiff-legged, offended way over snow. She is tiny and delicate, with long fluttering hands and long fluttering eyelashes. Her hair is brushed down her back in a curling cloak and she favours pale fabrics with soft, cloying textures: mohair, fake fur, fake suede. When she sits, she draws her wraps closer around her, peeps over the top of her fluffy scarf, smoothes down the nap of her velvety trousers. She needs, her gestures imply, some insulation from this grubby world: she is the princess continually pricked by peas. Also: she is a very well-wrapped parcel, a most expensive package; she must contain a jewel.

Nothing could be calculated to appeal more to Ahmed, a young German/Iraqi/Kurd (in what ratios is a matter of constant dispute) previously employed as pot-boy in the restaurant where Flora spent the summer working on reception, elevated on a swivel stool an elegant two feet above the common herd. If Flora is the pale lady from a Persian manuscript, he, dark-skinned and curly-haired, with flaring nostrils and urgent dark eyes, is her white-armoured swain. He follows her round town. He gets on the bus behind her. He sits on the wall outside the house – all night! The fact that he has picked up almost no English during what seems to be a least a year in this country is no object: Flora, who inherits her mother's gift for languages, speaks to him in her schoolgirl German, and rapidly acquires a thick Kurdish patois.

I can't see the problem; Antigona is appalled. Ahmed is courtly, romantic and careful, I point out, ideal first-boyfriend material. 'He is Muslim,' says Antigona. And it is true: Ahmed is a regular at the Wahabi mosque.

'But that means he isn't interested in drinking in nightclubs,' I counter.

'She is throwing away her school,' says Antigona. 'She is throwing away her future.'

'He's just a boyfriend,' I say, soothingly. 'Honestly, when I taught in a sixth-form college, loads of girls had boyfriends. They still got their A levels.'

'They were English,' says Antigona.

I remember some of those girls: the close single-mum-and-daughter pairings who would turn up at parents' evenings, wearing each other's clothes, giggling; the mother who was doing A levels with her daughter, a little spookily; the one who, more touchingly, confessed to reading all her daughter's set texts as she finished them. The sort of families where the boyfriend is petted and enthused about and allowed to move in, or at least eat dinner five times a week, until he realizes that he is not the first person in his girlfriend's life, and never will be. As a tactic for crushing the sexual instinct, that sort of smothering always struck me as supreme.

Antigona looks like one of those mothers now, with her assertive glitz and earrings. She has her jobs, her independence; she and Flora, rowing in their identical jeans, seem cute and kooky as Cher and Winona Ryder in that movie where they pretended to live in a trailer: I simply can't believe the opposition is serious. I let myself imagine that Antigona is merely playing the wicked stepmother in the story, paying lip-service to the Kanun by ritually objecting to all expressions of male interest in her daughter.

But she is much angrier than that. She is tired to the point of irrationality from her constant long hours, drained from her hopeless visit to Albania; hovering, in fact, on the brink of breakdown. The Kanun has her back, though she has switched from observed to observer. Several times a day, whenever there is a break in the schedule, she seizes her phone to inquire where Flora is and shout at her. She is obsessed, begging me over and over again to say that all Kurds are worthless and that Flora is throwing her life away and maybe she should be beaten or locked up.

I say, 'You should have him round to supper.'

'What?'

'You should have him round, get to know him, let them go out. Then she'll finish with him in a year or so, and she'll be able to move on.'

Whoosh! The blowtorch of Antigona's rage brushes over me, scorching my eyelashes. It's like when I ask her not to wash woollens with cottons – she simply thinks I'm being unclean. If she let Flora have a boyfriend she would be dirty. 'People from my culture' – she means her brothers – 'do not accept that,' she shouts. 'I employ you,' says a small, cold voice from my belly, and I shush it. My inner Pasha.

Antigona catches Flora and Ahmed walking down the High Street, and shouts abuse at them. She catches a rat in the restaurant and beats it to death with a broom. Her colour is constantly high, her hands constantly tense. She is making me nervous. To be precise, she is making me feel the way I did when I was seventeen, and in trouble with my mother. Antigona cleans with the same brooding menace.

Antigona's opposition has its inevitable effect: it ups the stakes. Soon, Flora comes round to negotiate, knowing I offer a measure of protection against her mother. She perches prettily on my sofa, and we start a strange, three-way conversation. 'Like *EastEnders*,' says Flora. 'You know, when they do issues,' and she's right: it's stagey, at first. All three of us keep giggling. We start off in English. Flora wants to get engaged to Ahmed. She will carry on with her studies. There is nothing to be afraid of. I back her up, hoping that 'engaged' might be a formula which would let the relationship run its natural course. Girls at my sixth-form college were always getting 'engaged', and flashing thin little rings. It didn't mean much. You could recycle the ring. But I am forgetting Antigona's own story, where 'engaged', 'married', 'raped', and 'a lifetime of servitude' all meant the same thing. The conversation soon moves beyond me, into terrible rage and shouted Albanian. Antigona is hunched over, shouting, as if she had been kicked in the stomach. I run away to the nursery, hear Flora slam out of the house.

'If you *don't* want them to get married you should let them get engaged,' I essay later, girlish and playful, trying to coax Antigona into a feminine conspiracy. I realize I'm anxious as a teenager myself. That I would do anything to appease her rage.

'She shouldn't do this to me. I did everything for her,' Antigona says, like all mothers, though with more truth than most.

'She's not doing it to you,' I say. 'She's just doing it.'

'That's the way you think here. English people. But that is not my culture,' says Antigona with such venom that I slip out of the room, because I can see that in a moment she will call me a prostitute, and I will respond with something like, 'No one owns anyone. Even if you did carry her out of a burning village on your back.' And we will both regret it. I am up against a true cultural difference here, a chasm between us on the nature of the individual. Antigona honestly regards

Flora as part of herself, not as a free agent at all. Perhaps all mothers feel like that about their daughters, but here the culture does not back them up.

The next day she tells me: 'I tell Flora to choose between him and me, her own mother.'

'What did she say?'

'She choose him. Can you believe that?'

I can, actually. 'So has she moved out?'

Of course not. The miserable affair rattles on, day to day. Antigona accepts Saturday and Sunday shifts at the restaurant. I begin to wonder if an Albanian compromise will be made, and the relationship will simply continue but be ignored, and so finally run its course. Mihane begins college, unnoticed. Flora's school term commences, but she is clearly not attending classes. Then one night Agim sticks in his inevitable oar. Prowling round in his taxi, he decides to check on his nieces. Ahmed is there in Flora's room. They are both fully clothed and studying the Koran; nevertheless Ahmed jumps out of the window (fortunately only ten feet to the nearest balcony) and is chased off by Agim. Flora, screaming, follows them both into the orange-lit night. Antigona is summoned home by Agim, but, by the time she gets there, her daughter has disappeared and cannot be contacted. Both her daughters, actually – Mihane has run off to her friend Laureen's. There is only Agim waiting for her in the kitchen, ready to threaten her and abuse her and tell her she and her daughters should be dead.

The next morning, Antigona staggers round to me, ashen and silent. She calls Mihane and begs her, at least, to come home. Later that day, Flora calls Mihane to say she is married, married in the mosque. For a few days, Antigona doesn't speak. Then she says she is going to Albania next week, do I mind. I cannot figure this as the most therapeutic of destinations; nevertheless, I get out the suitcase.

The day before she is due to leave, Flora comes round. She is dressed as a student, an English girl: hair in a ponytail, green parka jacket. She sits herself down on the sofa, elegant and self-possessed as ever. She is living with her 'husband' and 'another couple', she says, and has picked up her A levels again. She's come to ask me about the English syllabus. They are doing a play.

'Oh,' I say, 'Shakespeare?'

'No,' she says. 'I don't remember. Someone beginning with "W".'

Antigona comes in. She bungs the baby at me, shouts in Albanian. For a while, Flora sits on the sofa, replying in English, playing Patience on the Monument.

'Of course I love you, Mum. But I love my husband, too.'

'I'm still studying. He's very supportive.'

'He does have papers. He's German.'

'He doesn't want me to wear the scarf. He just doesn't like miniskirts.'

But the gravity, the primal magnetic pull of Antigona's Albanian rage, draws her in and they both start to shout, to and fro, with huge eloquent blazing speeches reminding me more than ever of watching the *Oresteia* in Russian. And it isn't till the last minute, when Antigona and Flora are both exhausted, are literally on the floor, on their knees, weeping, and Flora is about to leave – for the last time, of course, the last, as she is no longer Antigona's daughter – that I twig.

'Ah,' I say misremembering my Jacobeans. 'Webster. You're doing *The Revenger's Tragedy*!'

'No,' says Flora, fastening her parka, 'Not that one. The one about the Duchess.'

8
Albanian Stories

'This is Illyria, lady.'
William Shakespeare, *Twelfth Night*

Two weeks later, Antigona returns. And she has found her family, can you believe it?

I believe it. She has shed twenty years, she is pink-cheeked and bright-eyed, she is folk-dancing round the house with the gurgling baby: 'Nee, nee-nee nee, nee-nee, nee-nee-nee Nee!'

Here is how she did it. She had gone to Albania to meet a man. Since the trip to Vlores, it had been Albanians on Antigona's phone, imploring her to marry them – mostly for papers, she said. This one was particularly persistent. He kept begging her to visit him so he could demonstrate the seriousness of his intentions, and, mostly to get away from Flora and her brothers, she had consented. She realized she had made a mistake more or less at the airport, but he was desperate to close the deal. He wanted Antigona to visit his family. His home town was well up in the north, in the mountains towards the Montenegrin border.

Antigona calculated her options: this was the part of Albania she hadn't been able to visit the last time, because it was so lawless and unsafe. Travelling like this, in company with a man, even if he was a round-eyed idiot who kept licking his loose lower lip, was her only possible way of going there. She did not see why her family would have gone so far from their home as the North Albanian highlands; but then, she had travelled a long way herself, and she knew that only such an undocumented wilderness could conceal quite so many people for quite so long. Or a pit in the ground. Antigona was not going to consider pits in the ground: she stepped into the man's ancient Ford.

Together, they swore and hooted their way out of Mother Theresa Airport ('Mother Theresa', remember, is the answer to 'Name a Famous Albanian', that pleasant party alternative to 'Name a Famous Belgian'); drove through the bleak paved plains and mixed dictators' architecture, communist and fascist, of central Tirana (Antigona popped out to snap a self-portrait in the central square. She admires fascist architecture, to be honest); bumped and scratched past miles of luridly painted flats; then crawled through the unfinished roads and random half-built villas of the suburbs, the best of which look like the poorest parts of Sardinia or Naples, but with more children – flocks and flocks of children, some barefoot; out onto the flat, useless, reclaimed marshland where the wind whistles round more planned, useless concrete cities, up into the hills.

The *Montes*, says Antigona, smiling, for this is one noun for which she has refused the English: the vertiginous slopes, the scented forest, the fierce streams, the shining, scarred expanses of granite which are so particularly Albanian. She can't help being stirred by them. We took her to the Lake District once, and she turned into another creature, dashing up Coniston like a fell-runner. This part of Albania looks just like Kosovo – houses clinging to the slopes, pack-mules, beehives, hand-ploughs – except for the large concrete bunkers which disfigure even the most isolated corners. A bunker per Albanian, more or less. One of Hoxha's little fancies. As they wind up the tortuous hairpin bends, past the corpses of cars which didn't make it – really, pack-mules would be more practical – Antigona insists on stopping at every town and village hall and checking the register of inhabitants, looking for any mention of her family.

She is more or less out of hope when they finally see their destination: a grey heap of litter at the base of yet more soaring mountains. Close up, the town is an undistinguished, typically Albanian mixture of ancient stone and wattle houses and crumbling concrete flats: a sour, depopulated place mostly famous for its prison. Antigona was thoroughly fed up with the man by that time, disliked his stupid, cloying mother and sisters even more, and visited the town hall as much to escape them as anything. And there, in the handwritten register, perfectly plain, was her sister's name: Jehona. Widow. Seamstress. An address.

'Widow?' Yes. She lost her husband in the war. And her children. 'Her children?'

'She is crazy, actually. Mad.'

'How many children?'

'Two.'

'How?'

But Antigona is not going to linger here. She presses on.

'But my sister tell me where my mum is! She is living just outside the town. Five minutes, and I get in a taxi, minibus, and there she is. Imagine how surprised. She was outside, drying the corn, see, see, and I come up!'

Antigona shows me on her phone a sort of genre painting: an old woman with a white headscarf and a face so deeply lined it seems cracked, standing under a metallic sky, her brown hands full of corn. Fatmire, Antigona's mother. Not only was she living there, but also her sisters: Blerta, half a mile away; Vera, up a nearby mountain. Blerta is a widow, but not from the war: her husband died several years ago in a traffic accident and she is therefore saddled with her parents-in-law as well as her four children. Vera's three children have survived the war! And her husband, he of the dice, unfortunately. Antigona's father has made it, too, she says when I enquire, but he is less well – very silent.

But what are they doing there? How did they get there? Why did nobody know?

They just landed up there.

No, really. For once Antigona's vague, shrugged responses to my repeated direct questions are exact. It takes a very long time, more than a year, for me to extract the following account of the family's move. This is because it happened in the 'bad war', when things happened which no one can talk about, especially to Jehona. The detail which would have obsessed me, which is why their names appeared on none of the lists Antigona trawled through, seems to be of no interest to anyone. This family grew up under Tito and Milosevic; they have gone to live in Hoxha's ruined country: they do not expect justice from anyone, or information from lists.

When the NATO bombardment started, in the spring of 1999, Fatmire's daughters gathered at her house with their children. Blerta was long widowed, and had her parents-in-law with her. Jehona had just lost her husband and children in unspeakable circumstances. Vera's husband was with the KLA. Together, taking only what they could carry, the family joined the huge trail of people – you couldn't see where it began or ended – wandering at tractor pace towards the Macedonian border. This was the direction Antigona had expected them to take, because it was the direction of the only decent road. But a few hours into the family's journey, fate intervened in the shape of a lumbering bus. The coach, from a small Islamic relief agency, was there to take people to the Albanian border, which was further away but less crowded. By no means everyone wanted to go. Macedonia was a better economic option than Albania, and news had spread down the line that its border was open. Getting on the bus also necessitated leaving one's tractor behind, which meant abandoning many years of saving and hard labour. Fatmire's family had no tractor to lose, however. They climbed aboard, and more than a day later found themselves in Kukes, a bleak, entirely concrete town on the Albanian border where a huge UN refugee camp was well established.

Once in Albanian border country, we are in the land of estimates. Various refugee and news agencies reckon that nearly a million Kosovars crossed into Albania between April and June 1999. Officially, they all went back. But there are no figures or records of the thousands who, like Antigona, made their way to the coast of Albania and crossed to Italy, or the thousands more who walked to Greece, or got lorries to Germany or Denmark, or the many other thousands who, like Fatmire's family, got tired of the refugee camp, fanned out across the Albanian mountains, and simply settled down, sometimes with long-lost relatives. There were some official Albanian programmes to promote this, but Antigona's family doesn't seem to have been part of them.

The resettlement, official or not, was possible because the mountains were depopulated. Since the Albanian popular revolution of 1992, when the borders were opened, and particularly since the pyramid-selling disaster of 1997, when many Albanians lost their savings and pensions, anyone who had any possibility of earning hard currency had left the country. At least a quarter of the population of Albania now lives abroad, and the exodus from the highlands was even heavier than that, because the able-bodied from there also went to Tirana. The mountains were therefore littered with crumbling smallholdings and remains of collective farms which nominally belonged to a cousin or an uncle abroad. Many Kosovars, having seen their own villages burnt, made themselves at home in the Albanian vacancies. Of course. They *were* at home: Fatmire grew up only thirty miles from where she has now settled, and soon discovered some cousins in the nearby town. This was still the Malësi, the ancestral mountains, where people spoke the ancestral tongue and followed the ancestral Kanun. Besides, though the world might reckon them ignorant and backward, they, and they alone, knew how to wrench a living from the harsh landscape of granite and forest.

Work. I suspect Fatmire turns to it as Antigona does, letting its steady hammer-blows fill her head in order to exclude the voices and the questions: where were her sons, Agim, Driton and little Hasan? Had they ever reached Italy? While she is ploughing a terrace left fallow for four years, standing on a blade pulled by a bullock, smashing the knotted turf with a hoe and then her hands, she will have no time to think of that. Where was her beautiful daughter Antigona and her children? As long as she is repairing a drystone wall the thought will not occur. What had happened to the village she had lived in for forty-five years? Where had her near neighbours gone, her sisters-in-law, her cousins, the butcher, the baker, the candlestick-maker? If there are new neighbours to bargain with, a cow to be got on credit, there will be no time to speculate. And Jehona's little boys, Alban and Djon – eleven and six, the little scamps, all bright eyes and elbows in Fatmire's hand-knits – where were they? Time for another cigarette, another coffee (Fatmire smokes like a man, and knocks back great snifters of raki, too), then on with hammering in the fence-post, with dragging buckets from the well on a yoke. What happened to

Jehona – who has taken to washing her hands twenty times a day, scrubbing them till they bleed – during the outrage no one can talk about? Where was she when her children died? Walk. Walk up the mountain to mend the fence, down to bring in the cows. If you walk enough, sleep is dreamless.

Fatmire is sixty years old, and for most of her life she worked on a collective farm. The collective ideas, she thinks, were generally bad. They had no feeling for cows. You need a relationship with a cow if the creature is to produce milk. At least this is hers, this land, her smallholding, her crops. She has ploughed and fenced every foot of it herself. Her husband is up the mountain, tending the white donkey. The donkey is a bloody useless donkey, well past ploughing, mostly past carrying loads, but the old man spends hours with it, looking into its sad dark eyes, feeding it grass, giving it the cows' feed, even greens from the terrace. Fatmire is considering getting up in the night and turning it loose. They can't afford pets.

After four years of unremitting work, Fatmire once again has a flourishing smallholding and three cows. One of Vera's boys, who lives with her, takes the milk every day to sell in town. Further up the mountain, the indomitable Blerta has two cows and many chickens. Vera, further up still, has sheep. Her husband doesn't play dice since the war: in fact, he very rarely comes down from his mountain peak at all, so obsessed is he with his gun and his boarhounds; and his temper is more vicious than ever. Vera escapes only rarely to see her mother and son, but she is there to help gather in the corn. So is Blerta. So all three are together, splitting the milky ears with a long knife, laying them to dry on a clean cloth on the roof of the stable, when the minibus draws up and their dead sister Antigona issues from it: Persephone fresh from the underworld; a place, clearly, where women dress in white jeans and gold grows on trees.

They cannot believe it. They grasp her in their cracking hands, pull her strangely moist, youthful cheek to their burnt faces, inhale her perfume, push her back to gaze again, weep and weep. They cannot believe it, they cannot believe it. It is the happiest moment of their lives. Antigona waves her phone above their heads like a stiff, beneficent angel, and takes their picture all together.

Antigona was able to make only one more trip to Albania before her travel rights ran out: a triumphant four-week holiday, with Ylli, in the summer of 2005. But she is constantly in touch, for she found her family at around the same time as mobile phone masts were first heaved up the Accursed Mountains. The network soon worked far better than anything else in the area, and many inhabitants of drystone and wattle farmhouses without sewage or running water suddenly found themselves equipped to talk to the sons and daughters abroad who were keeping the show on the road, and to send instant pictures of themselves, too, if the fancy took them.

There are problems, of course – when the generator runs dry and the phone can't be charged, and when phonecards which promise ninety minutes deliver forty-five – but generally, for a price roughly equivalent to a return air ticket per month, Antigona is able to join in, day and night, the conversation of her mothers and sisters. As she slides the pushchair round Tesco, she can tuck her phone under her chin and chat to Vera among her flock; while she pushes the toddler's swing, she can talk to Blerta pumping water from her well; as she takes the bus to the restaurant at night, she can ring to complain of her daughters, and her mother will rage and weep with her and attempt to read their fate in the near, alarming Albanian stars.

This is what Antigona has been missing, above all: this endless conversation. Every action, every encounter, every gift, every bargain, reported, foreseen, commended, condemned, nothing kept back, no relationship private, the mother the centre of all. Passionate and often flirtatious as Antigona is, she does not, I now realize, expect any kind of emotional interchange from men: all her life, love, support and understanding has come only from women. She is hugely happy, despite her troubles with her daughters, to be restored to it. Now she is a widow among widows (no one seems to have registered her divorce), and a powerful person, too, the richest of her sisters, Jack back from the beanstalk with all the giant's treasure.

On goes the talk, the Albanian shouts and purrs and exclamations and roaring laughter: a part of Antigona is back on her native mountains, waiting by the well for her sisters, walking her mother into town. The stories which follow are drawn from this talk. From the outset, Antigona includes me in it: she asks me if I don't think eighteen euros (all prices are in hard currency, euros and dollars remitted by relatives abroad) for a Turkish knit jumper isn't an outrageous price – I agree heartily; she tells me when Fatmire's new calf is born. I follow, over two years, the agonizing progress of Vera's sons, as they attempt, over and over again, to cross the Greek border, and are brutally turned back by the border police. It's a good thing I kept a diary; otherwise the proper sequence of events might be hard to establish, because, in the talk, legends are quickly made, characters, myth. Things are as they should be, rather than as they are.

Dates are difficult, too: when she first came to this country, Antigona found calendars and timekeeping nearly impossible. She has learned, of course, as she learns everything, but her talk with her mother still happens in an Albanian time frame, where there are tomorrows but very few names of months or years. Fatmire, who holds as many tasks in her head as a busy building-site manager, and schedules her days with as much precision, would have to count on her fingers to tell you how many years it is since she left Kosovo, in the same way that speakers of Scots Gaelic have to break into English to name a date or put a number on a year.

Talk, talk. No wonder Flora despaired, and ran off: her mother expects all this of her, expects her to give herself up to her as Antigona, Blerta and Vera are given up to Fatmire. For is this not how mothers and daughters should be? Remarkable as Fatmire is, fount of life and ingenuity though she be, is not Antigona just as extraordinary, deserving of just as much from her daughters? Who pulled them from the fire? Who put them on the lifeboat?

In school, from the television, from their peers, Mihane and Flora have learnt different ideas. They chat about other topics on their mobile phones.

Jehona and the Giant Baby

It is winter 2005, a year after Antigona first found her family. Antigona and I are peering at my telly. It is running a short, rather crackly video tape showing a jolly, fat baby having a bath in a plastic sink, sitting on a double bed covered with teddies, being dressed in a ludicrous lacy garment, munching a plate of polenta and finally toddling round a concrete-floored room with the bow-legged stagger of the child who has just learned to walk. I say, of course, that she is gorgeous. She is. I try to find other ways of saying it. But Antigona is not blessing the little one or giggling with pleasure or remarking on her precocious handling of the spoon, or doing any of the rest of her usual baby performance. Antigona is staring at the screen, frozen-faced. I give up.

'She's at least a year old,' I say. 'Got to be.'

'I know,' she says. 'I always knew it.' Her face draws in, stiff and toothless. I know that crone face, all too well. It is the face of the Kanun of Lek, and it smells shame.

You see, according to Jehona's account, her baby

should be only seven months old. Officially, the little one was born in the spring, in Greece, where Jehona was, officially, living with her new husband, a man called Ari. There had been a flurry of phone calls at the time. The baby was born in hospital, by Caesarean, two months early. And she was said a few days later to be suffering from gigantism. When Antigona reported this to me, in some distress, I looked it up. The outlook, I had to tell her, was bleak. Gigantism is very unusual, far rarer than dwarfism, and with much more serious impacts on health and life expectancy. I was very sorry. It seemed monstrous to me that Jehona, who had lost two children and been through so much to bear a third, should give birth to so seriously handicapped a child. But, said Antigona, Jehona was now reporting that the baby would be OK. They were going to give her some injections, and she would be normal. Just a bit big for her age. I did not at all see how this could be, but I knew better than to argue with Antigona, who was giving me one of her looks. A translation problem, we agreed. But now:

'That baby,' says Antigona, 'is one hundred per cent normal. She is gorgeous. She is one years old.'

'So you think that maybe she was born last autumn . . . ?'

'She was pregnant! Jehona was. Last year. When I found her! I'm sure, I am one hundred per cent certain. I said to her, "You are pregnant" – remember, I told you about it – you are pregnant, I said, and she was very angry with me, she said, "No, I am fat, not everyone is as thin as you." Bitch.'

'But she walked over the mountains,' I protest. 'Last autumn. She couldn't have been giving birth. She was walking to Greece.'

'She *said*,' says Antigona.

A couple of months after Antigona returned from her triumphant first trip to Albania, Jehona rang out of the blue and announced she was coming to England, courtesy of some people-smugglers. Antigona was horrified on several grounds: people-smugglers are not to be trusted; she didn't want to break the law while her own papers were up for renewal; she couldn't afford to support Jehona . . .

'You could find her cleaning work?' I suggested at the time. Antigona tossed her head.

'She cannot clean! To be cleaner, you have to clean toilets! Jehona is very hygienic, she is crazy hygienic! You sit down in her house, she wash the cushions! She is crazy about germs! You ask her for coffee, she can't come for coffee because she is cleaning the house. She is cleaning the door! She is cleaning the window! She is cleaning the door handle.'

Jehona has obsessive compulsive disorder, it sounded like. I had to agree this is not promising in a Maid. And what else? Why was Antigona so very angry?

'I never like her. Of all my sisters, she is the one you do not trust. We are not close. She never give anything. She take, always take.'

'What has she taken?'

'Like clothes and things. Those boots I send to Albania, for Blerta's daughter? She take them.'

'What else?'

Well, Antigona's life savings, it turns out. The money she calls 'my sweat'. The money from the restaurant. The money she was keeping back, in case she got deported.

'About £10,000?' I said, having done some secret sums.

'Exactly.'

When Antigona first went to Albania, she found Jehona living hand to mouth in an impenetrable web of petty deceptions and debt. It was inevitable. Jehona was trying to do the impossible: to make a living as a seamstress in a town where there were almost no wages, where all cash was sent from abroad; and to live independently as a woman in a society in thrall to the Kanun of Lek. Jehona is not tough, she is not Blerta or Fatmire, she was always inclined to fib and gossip in corners and hang to the side. Moreover, since her 'bad war', she is, as Antigona baldly states, more or less insane, liable to spend days scrubbing her house and her hands in thrall to her obsessive compulsive disorder. Here, she would certainly be on disability benefit: there, she had got herself into a state where, just a week or so after Antigona found her, and probably not unrelated to the sudden appearance of a moneyed sister, her little flat was about to be repossessed by men with guns.

Antigona, after much thought and some terrific shouting matches, paid them off. This completely cleaned her out: for the first time since she settled her debt to her brothers, she had nothing in the bank. She knew that Jehona would never be able to pay back any of the cash, so she asked to be considered the owner of the disputed flat instead. The flat had a small shop attached, and Antigona hoped that Blerta and Fatmire might stock it with their produce. The flat and shop could help her family and also be Antigona's security in Albania should she be deported. And she had saved her sister's life: altogether, money well spent.

Except that just a month later, in November, Jehona phoned to say she was on her way to England. She had mortgaged Antigona's flat and given the money to people-smugglers. Antigona's good deed, her schemes for her sisters, her security, and the money she had worked for day and night for years, were all gone; gone in forty-eight hours, in hock forever to unknown armed Albanians. No wonder Antigona was furious. But Jehona never showed up here. She rang instead from, she said, Greece. She said she had walked all the way there and then been abandoned by the people-smugglers. She raved about having appendicitis and being in hospital. And Antigona, with gritted teeth, sent more money.

Later, Jehona rang with good news. She had met an Albanian called Ari. She was going to marry him. She had found a job as a nanny, just like Antigona – listen, the baby crying in the background. And, guess what, she was pregnant! Ten months later, she turned up back at her mother's house with the giant baby, the baby who was six months old but starting to walk. A miracle! Gigantism! Fatmire had sent the video.

'But I think,' says Antigona, dark and sour, 'I think she never even went to Greece. Maybe she just went to the south. South Albania. Just somewhere to have her baby hidden.'

'With Ari?'

'Ari! He doesn't exist, Ari! No one has seen him! Where is he?'

'I thought he spoke on the phone that time to your Mum?'

'She just pull someone in from the street, I think. Just, hello, who are you, speak to my Mum please! You know? Since she come back to my Mum, he hasn't phoned, nothing.'

'Then who is the father of the child?'

'The same guy as before.'

'What guy?'

'A guy in the city. He is policeman – married. Children. Everything.'

'She's been seeing him on the side?'

'She has done this before!' Antigona blurts out, scarlet.

'Done what before?'

'Got pregnant.'

'Got pregnant?'

'Yeah. Year before last, she did. With this guy. The policeman. She was planning to have the baby. Can you bclicvc it? But my mum and Blerta found out in time, so they took her to another city, and . . .' Antigona gestures outwards from her stomach, as if pulling a long scarf from her belt.

'They made her have an abortion?'

'Yeah.'

'Why?'

'Because of shame! Because of opinion! Kate, you don't know what it is like, there.'

I don't know what it is like, there. But I have stopped nodding, stopped supporting. I am open-mouthed. I am thinking about Jehona, the plump, shifty, hare-faced woman of Antigona's photographs, thrust in the back of a tin van with Blerta on one side, Fatmire on the other, rattling over the mountains to have a late abortion, the kind where you give birth, where you see the stillborn tiny child, translucent and lifeless as a doll. Her mother and her sister did that to her, to a woman who had had her children taken away and shot, or maybe not even taken away, perhaps just shot; they had done that to her because they were ashamed.

'What do you think?'

Antigona wants my response. My unqualified support, I know. But I am thinking that I don't want any more babies fed to the toothless maw of the Kanun of Lek, that I want Jehona's new baby to live, and her preposterous, gigantic fiction with it.

'But her babies died, Antigona,' I say. 'Jehona's children. Her little boys. They died in the war.'

'That's what she always says,' says Antigona bitterly. 'Then she just cries, and makes no sense.'

We don't know what happened to Jehona's sons and husband in the war, because she has never said and her family don't ask. When the Serb paramilitaries came to villages, they generally separated the able-bodied men from the women and children, then took away and sometimes killed the men and made the women and children refugees by burning their property. This accords with the rules of the Kanun of Lek: houses may be burned and any number of men killed, but women are sacred. But there are reports of young boys and old men being taken when there were no able-bodied men to be found, and shot. There are also reports of whole village populations, entire clans right down to babes in arms, being lined up and shot and then buried in cattle pits. There are reports of barns full of villagers being torched. And there are many, many reports of women being separated from their children and assaulted, of being raped on pain of their children being killed, of being raped in public, of being gang-raped, of groups of women being kept naked in barns and forced to serve the Serbs food and drink while naked and then being gang-raped: as if once the mountain law was broken, the men were compelled to go further and further into their transgression.

'Antigona,' I say. 'What if Jehona was raped? You know, in the war?'

'Then it is shame on them,' says Antigona.

'Shame on the Serbs?'

'No. Shame on my family. Just the same as this shame. As having a bastard child.'

'Just the same?'

Antigona nods, her eyes half-closed, breathing narrowly.

Rape, the reports say, is particularly difficult for women from traditional families, like Jehona. They are unable to report it, because of shame. Because women are always complicit in sexual activity, and must be punished – like the kidnapped, trafficked girl Antigona told me about, shot in the public square by her brothers, because of shame. Jehona must remember the deaths of her children, she must remember it all the time, but she cannot speak about it, because of shame. Her family don't ask; don't want to know, because of shame. Because of shame, the narrowed eyes and toothless mouth of shame, the mask I see passing over Antigona's face, the mask that must have been on Blerta's and Fatmire's faces the day they came to take Jehona for the abortion.

'Jehona always think she is so clever. She always think she knows better than us. She always follow her own idea,' says Antigona.

'That,' I announce crisply, 'is exactly what they all say about you. Now, isn't it?'

Antigona laughs. She is calming down. Explaining the thing to me reminds her that in fact, she has grown away from the Kanun. What she says next makes perfect sense.

'She is forty-three. She is not strong, she is not clever. She wants a child, OK, she lost her children. Here you do not mind, but here you have benefits and things. Single mum. But, there, who will raise that child? My Mum and Blerta. And who is going to pay for the child? Me. Because when Agim finds out – he'll shoot her.'

I know this is true. I know that Antigona has already given Jehona, her least close, least giving, least sympathetic sister, everything she owns and has worked for. It is unreasonable of me to expect more, and more unreasonable still to expect Antigona to find feminist solidarity with Jehona because they have both, perhaps, found out the evils of the Kanun of Lek while being violently raped. Antigona can't analyse the situation like that. Or rather, she can, but she cannot sustain the thought or feel it in her body. Antigona needs to feel 'clean' in the sense of the Kanun, or her life is intolerable to her. Part of feeling 'clean' is expelling dirt, even, or especially, when the dirt is near you. Antigona would certainly have put Jehona on that van. She will never ask her how her children died.

And yet, and yet . . . The video has been frozen for twenty minutes, Jehona's dark-haired daughter, one lock of hair in a preposterous bow, staring up at us.

'It isn't the baby's fault,' I say.

'She is angel,' says Antigona, shaking her head. 'She do not ask to come to this world.'

She turns off the TV, takes the video out of the machine, and removes the mini camera cassette from its casing. Then, deliberately, she tugs the tape out, nicks it with a kitchen knife, slices it down the middle, and pulls, reducing it to celluloid ringlets.

She was supposed to pass the video to Agim. Now –

'I'll say it was the machine,' says Antigona.

Jehona's daughter is named Jolie. I ask what it means, hoping for another glorious, uniquely Albanian derivation. Jehona's own name means 'echo', and I assume she would like to reach beyond this for an optimistic name, one of the many in Albanian which promise spring and renewal: Drita (light), Blerta (green) or Lindita (dawn). Surely she'd want something gorgeous for the little girl with the ridiculous bow, a name which reflects the pantheist absorption in nature which is the most attractive aspect of Albanian culture: Flutura, perhaps, which means butterfly, or Lule, flower, even Era (snow). I love the ancient Greek names still in use in Albanian, the ones which reflect the people's claim to be the original Illyrians, the last tribe of the ancient world still living an ancient life: Antigona's own magnificent moniker, of course, but Afrodita, too, or Daphina, Andronika, Ariadna . . .

But Jolie, it turns out, is for Angelina, the film star. Jehona read it in a magazine. Antigona says the old names are going rapidly out of style. A generation of fathers patriotically named Alban and Bashkim (Albanian, Unity) and mothers named Besarta and Elira (Golden Promise, Freedom), are giving their children Western names and names made up from their parents initials, so that Alban and Besarta's son is called Abi, for example, which means nothing beyond itself.

Antigona cannot understand why this should depress me. There are, she says, far more serious things to worry about in Albania, such as inflation and the exchange rate and corruption and the roads. Can I imagine what it is like to earn £75 a month as a nurse but to live in a world where prices are the same as European ones? Because that is what has happened in northern Albania. All cash is imported, and cash prices are imported too, so anything you do not grow or make yourself is vastly expensive. Vera's daughter wants to train as a nurse, but what, honestly, is the point? They'd have to pay a big bribe to get her started on scrubbing the hospital floors. You have to pay bribes for everything, in euros, especially to the police. 'Nothing is clear there,' says Antigona. People there are stuck, stuck in their lives, stuck in the useless roads.

I know Antigona is mostly right. How can I expect Albanians to treasure their language when the world condemns it as the code of thieves? Why do I think Albanians should repair their ancient mule-paths and get back on their horses when I tut over minor potholes in our metalled roads? It's like objecting to the corrugated iron Agim has paid for to mend Blerta's – to my mind – exquisite ancient farmhouse: aesthetic, indulgent, sentimental. And yet . . . surely the names reflect a level of national shame, national self-abasement?

If it was oppressive and often terrifying to be an Albanian for most of the twentieth century then at least it was no worse than this warlike nation was used to, no more than they'd always lived with. But in 1992 this pathologically proud people woke from the long dream of Hoxha's Maoist state to find themselves more degraded than embattled: the poorest nation in Europe, the one with least infrastructure, the most laughable telly, the worst football team, the most alien language, the least polyglot and educated population. The pyramid-selling disaster of '97 bankrupted and also disgraced them: now they were the nation which lost its entire savings over something as obviously pie-in-the-sky as a chain letter. A quarter of the Albanian population now lives abroad, absorbing the world's view of them: pariahs, bywords for criminality and stupidity. For men as exquisitely proud and immaculately honest as Agim, Hasan, and Driton, mountain men, raised to be huntsmen, elders of the *fis*, this must be a sort of daily torture. And it must account, too, I suppose, for the number of babies no longer called 'Freedom', for the children named instead for Hollywood, or after the parents whose greatest accomplishment is simply to survive.

Blerta's Daughter

Here is what a mobile phone can do: it can link Antigona, bouncing to Tesco one fine October morning in her new high-rise trainers, to Blerta, walking down a mountain with two chickens on her head and nothing but a plastic flip-flop between her foot and the cobbled path. Not that it hurts: Blerta is hoof and horn. Antigona once heard my husband refer to 'those old women you always find in southern Italian villages', and corrected him: 'They are not old, actually. They are forty.' Blerta's age. Blerta is wearing, as she has all her life, baggy Turkish trousers under a heavy skirt. Her head is wrapped in a white scarf like her mother's – this is no longer socially required of widows, but Blerta prefers it, for she cares nothing for fashion – and her nutcracker face is nearly as brown and grooved. Antigona, they tell her in the restaurant, looks 'twenty-two from behind'. She knows it. She twinkles down Stoke Newington High Street, drawing every eye in her lush pink velour tracksuit.

Antigona has rung Blerta on impulse. It's usually a

cheap call: Blerta is busy and taciturn. Today, though, she wants to talk. She has been regretting the slaughter of the chickens for nearly two of Antigona's expensive minutes. They were young chickens, with more growing to do. They might have been layers, if she had left them to it. She might have sold them later, for more money. Or they might have been the family feast, at New Year. But today is market day, and Blerta needs the money.

Antigona changes the subject. Her sisters' poverty is nearly unbearable to her. 'Which one to help?' she says to me, constantly. 'Everyone she need it.' Bribes for doctors, teachers, policemen; money for medicines, clothing, nappies; a cot for baby Jolie, found sleeping on concrete in November: a fathomless hole has opened in Antigona's life, a Sisyphean hill grown up. So today Antigona swiftly asks after her niece. That usually cheers Blerta up.

For Blerta's daughter, the austerely named Mersela (March), is a most extraordinary person. What on earth, say the sisters to each other, as they always say to each other, as Antigona often rehearses to me (though always with the tag that Flora has better chances and does nothing with them), can have possessed the child? How can it even have occurred to this tiny, pale girl, who even at nineteen has no breasts and no hips and wears her hair in a long hard plait, this silent, soup-eyed, tight-lipped child who goes through agonies of embarrassment every time the family have to pay respects to the dead, who is paralysed with mortification when her mother makes her hand round the baklava at the feast afterwards, that she would want to take herself alone to the University of Tirana to study Arts and Literature?

There is something inside Mersela, Antigona says, laying it on thick for me, a special family spirit. How else could an orphan, a child who saw her father killed when she was five, a refugee, a girl who spent most of her fourteenth year trekking across the Albanian mountains, a peasant, someone who never owned a book, who went only to the simplest schools, who worked every night on the land till she dropped – how else could such a girl get the highest mark in the School Certificate in the entire region? Brains, say the sisters to each other, the family brains. And ingenuity, persistence, persistence, and hard, hard work.

No one, says Antigona, no slouch herself, could work harder than Blerta. She wakes at four every morning and goes out to the chickens, the cows, the rabbits, the well. I imagine her moving, not with Fatmire's deceptive smooth slowness, steady and effective as a tortoise's chew, but in tigerish pounces like Antigona, a furious shaking of each task to death. Blerta, like Antigona, had only primary education, and she was taught moreover for the first couple of years in Serbo-Croat, but she is clever, says Antigona, 'clever like three times Uni'. Blerta feeds three adults and four teenagers off a few stony terraces. She must understand very well the satisfaction Mersela found in learning Chemistry without a test tube, English without a speaker in miles, History from Hoxha-era textbooks: it is the satisfaction of wringing the last drop of water from the rag, of picking the last grain of corn from the soil. In her conversations with her sister, at least, it is a satisfaction she takes for her own.

Mersela started her course in 2004, at the same time as Antigona found her family. Antigona is hugely proud of her and carefully keeps me up with her progress. Mersela lives in the college. She shares a room with five other girls: a room with six beds, a tap and a stove. She eats only what she can cook there: polenta, eggs from her mother. She never goes out into Tirana, not even for a coffee, for she is terrified, apart from the money question, of being raped and kidnapped. She is horrified by some of her room-mates who wear short skirts and bleach their hair, and is rather a figure of fun among the rest – the country girl who always works too hard, whose essay you can copy, though she will watch as you do, tight-lipped with rage. They mock her accent: Mersela is a Gheg speaker from the north, while most of the university girls speak the southern Tosk form of Albanian. Her marks in English, and in all oral exams, are not good because of the way she talks. Once, Antigona reports to me with glee, she stayed behind after class, and challenged the teacher: why only a six for me, and an eight for her? I gave more answers; I was correct, not her, though she has the pretty voice, she is from the south, and the teacher, stunned by the impact of the family rage, raised her mark. At the end of the year, Mersela had an average of eight out of ten: good, very good. Mersela can stay on, she can train to be a teacher, she can contemplate a future wage of £3,000 a year.

But that brings us back to the chickens. Money, again. The first year of the course, Blerta borrowed money from a businessman in town for the fees, and raised Mersela's living expenses herself. This year, though, the businessman wants three times the interest, because Blerta's family have been found and he knows Blerta has a source of hard cash. But the brothers won't give any money for Mersela's course – only to repair Blerta's farmhouse. They don't think Mersela should be alone in Tirana, because of Shame. Blerta felt their disapproval bitterly: so did Antigona. But Antigona couldn't help, either, just then. Since she paid Jehona's debts, she has been unable to save more than a few hundred pounds at a time, and she had just footed a medical bill for her mother.

Nevertheless, Mersela must have her chance. Blerta sold a cow and paid the first instalment of fees. She had no idea where the next instalment would come from and she could give Mersela only £25 to live on. But Mersela swore she could get by on that till the end of term. She said her mother mustn't worry, she would do very well on cornmeal and eggs; she could borrow books, she would phone. But Blerta did worry, and when she had on impulse called the girl the previous afternoon, and caught her at a low moment, she was perfectly well able to understand that Mersela had nothing left, that she was actually very hungry and scared. Blerta is scared too. So she is doing the only thing she can think of: selling the chickens. They will make perhaps £5. She will give the money to a friend's cousin, who is going to Tirana – and then, what?

Blerta can't go to Tirana herself. It's not just the time and the money; it's her parents-in-law. She did accompany Mersela the first time, mustered all her pride in order to walk – the very picture of a peasant, she knew – carrying Mersela's bundle, through the streets of Tirana, past the portals of the grand Italian Fascist College all the way to that miserable room. When she came back, her parents-in-law denounced her as a prostitute, and spent the next market day and all of the New Year Feast telling anyone who would listen that Blerta had a lover in Tirana.

'Can't she just ask them to leave?' I ask Antigona of these parents-in-law. Blerta literally carried her mother-in-law out of Kosovo. She has grown, cooked and laid before them three meals a day for twenty years. They sleep in the best room of the house. 'I mean, if they treat her like that.'

'No,' says Antigona. 'Her husband he die, so she have to look after the parents, it is tradition. Anyway, if she go, if she move in with my mum, they get her farm. The old man. Four years of her sweat.'

'Because Blerta can't own property?'

'She is their property. Her parents-in-law. She belongs to them.'

'Couldn't she just, like, murder them or something?'

Antigona thinks that is an excellent suggestion, and passes it on to Blerta. Tie them in a sack! says Antigona on the phone. Roll them into the river! And Blerta laughs at her little sister, as she always has, and tells her off.

The parents-in-law don't want to help Mersela, of

course. They think she should get married. It often seems to Blerta she is the only person in the world who wants to help Mersela. The people in the market do not want to help Mersela. They look coldly on her chickens laid out on a cloth in front of her, they offer her laughable prices. Blerta is angry: she forgets to banter, she lets real rage enter her voice while haggling. The customers notice, and drift away. It takes her too long to sell the chickens, and she gets only £3 for them. Then she has to run to meet the friend's cousin at the cafe where the minivans go. She is late, she is sweating, she has chicken blood on her skirt, and she has to wade into a cafe full of men and cigarette smoke. She has met the man only once – she looks around and around and he is not there, and she has to bear much mockery and laughter before she finds out that, actually, he left an hour ago. Which is when Blerta, for the first time in her life, calls England, and pours out the whole story to Antigona, who is by then at work and able to relay the tale to me.

I, in turn, call Jeannie. A dishwasher from Antigona's restaurant is going to Tirana the next week: a reliable courier. So Jeannie and I get £500 in £20 notes from the cashpoint, and interleave it in a copy of *My Antonia*. (We argued over this. I wanted to send *Anne of Green Gables*; Jeannie voted for *Claudine À L'École*.) We wrap the book into a parcel, and write Mersela's name firmly on the front.

Neither of us gives much to charity, usually – but this is so much more fun. This is almost dangerously much fun: it is nearly enough to make me forget about the overarching political injustice of my wealth and Mersela's poverty. It is such a lovely thought, the crisp notes falling out of the book, the money exactly where we most approve. We collect instant, tearful gratitude from Blerta and Mersela – and of course from Antigona. Though Antigona is just a little bitter, a little wistful – Mersela is just Flora's age, she is dressed entirely in Flora's cast-offs. Flora was supposed to go to university, and now it seems she never will.

I thought – and so, I suspect, did Antigona – that the joy of finding the family would unite Antigona with her brothers and with Flora. After all, when Antigona burst in upon her mother and sisters, she brought not only herself but news of her brothers, lost since 1998. Surely such a grand resurrection would outweigh Flora's sin in marrying Ahmed. But when Antigona calls her brothers from Albania, Agim does not forget his grudge against his niece. He is angry with Antigona for travelling alone, too, and suspicious of the man in the terrible car. After wasting many minutes on cross-questioning her, he decides to speak only to Fatmire and Blerta, not to Antigona, and not, when he has found out only a little about her life, to Jehona. When she gets back to London, Antigona finds that Hasan and even Driton have been recruited to his cause. She is excommunicated, as are Mihane and Ylli. Flora doesn't exist, and in fact Agim will never allow her name to be mentioned to him again for as long he is resident in this country.

For Agim's male pride is insulted, as well as the rest.

As the oldest son, he should have been the one to find and support his mother: the fact that his moneyed, empowered sister did so is deeply hurtful for him. It makes things much worse that his Leave to Remain has run out, and there has been no Home Office response to his application for more time: he cannot visit Albania to see for himself; all he can do is remit money and shout down the phone. Driton's papers are legal, though, thanks to his recent Spanish marriage, and Driton, accompanied by his wife, shortly sets off for Albania. When he comes back, he immediately, urged on by the excellent Maria, calls his sister to discuss what to do, who to help. This fraternal disobedience only adds to Agim's frustrations, however, as does the fact that in the spring after the family are discovered, it is only Driton who has the papers to invite his parents over to England for a special event: Hasan is getting married.

Hasan? Yes. After a long, a very long, period on Era's sofa, Hasan roused himself and went to work in a pizza restaurant as a kitchen assistant. Here he displayed an almost alarming aptitude for doing exactly as he was asked in total silence, and was shortly promoted to assistant chef: which meant assembling the pizzas from the order board at great speed, cooking each to a turn, and never, never failing to put together a group order as a group. Again, Hasan proved himself sublimely silent and efficient. So talented has he grown, in fact, that he has been offered a new job: pizza chef in a new branch in London Fields. Very long hours, but he can live in the tiny flat above the restaurant, with his new wife, the blonde, the wobbly, the – as Antigona sourly points out – moustached and rather dim, but English, fully English with full papers, Jennifer. Softened by his approaching nuptials, Hasan takes Jennifer to meet Antigona in a cafe in Stoke Newington, and apologizes for the fact that, of course, he can't ask her to the wedding. Jennifer sympathizes with Antigona over her daughter, which on the whole she finds rather insulting.

Antigona nonetheless starts happily window-shopping for the wedding. There is a dress in Zara she likes, and another in New Look. She tells me that Agim will hardly be able to stop her attending the party when her parents are staying with her. And her parents will have to stay in her house, because she is the only one with a spare room. She is hugely excited about their arrival. She buys new sheets, huge quantities of food. The day of their arrival she even takes the day off work, which is unheard of. The next morning, however, she arrives pale and sick, sits on the floor, weeps, and tells me this story.

Driton met his parents at Heathrow and drove them straight to Antigona's, where a great feast of meats, salads, baklava, several kinds of fruit juice and Coke were laid out. The old couple sat down and ate hugely, gazing in awe around them at the shiny sofas, the Argos glass ornaments, the antique lamp. Antigona shows me the phone-photos: the old man skinny and bald, his wife with long hair covered with a white scarf, both of them in funeral suits. After the meal, they lit cigarettes and filled the room with the weedy

Albanian fug, they unfurled their cracked working hands into the strange airless central heating, and Fatmire was about to say again it is all marvellous, what amazing roads they drove down, better a dog in this country than a man at home, when Agim and Era turned up at the door.

Fatmire was overwhelmed with joy to see her son, to meet her daughter-in-law, to kiss her grandchildren. Antigona was poised for the grand reconciliation – but Agim had not come for any such thing. Solemnly, in front of his parents, he denounced and shamed his sister. She is a loose woman, he said; she had, in defiance of him, worked in a restaurant, and as a result, her daughters were lost to shame. He and his family cannot associate with her, and he will not visit his mother as long as she stays in her house. Fatmire weeps and screams: she will stay with her daughter. The old man, Afrim, sinks his head into his hands and weeps too. Agim holds himself as tall as a short fat man can manage and delivers his final riposte.

'She is your eldest son, now,' he says, pointing to Antigona, and he walks out of the room. At the door he turns to make sure Driton is coming, too. Driton, who has been looking hard at the carpet for the past half-hour, kisses his mother, and does so.

So misery is added to misery and disgrace to disgrace, layer on layer on yellowing layer – like the pee stains on Antigona's best mattress, in fact. For Afrim develops a terrible infection of the bladder which makes him incontinent. Antigona is full of furious blame, but a visit to the doctor points to a major underlying problem which can't be investigated here because of lack of health insurance. Afrim spends the rest of his time in London lying in bed and smoking, and shouting at everyone except Ylli, to whom, like the rest of the world, he has taken a fancy.

Fatmire tries, meanwhile, to get something out of her stay. She comes to work with Antigona and admires the pretty blonde children, then weeps when they lisp her name: it is her grandchildren, Agim's daughters, who should be doing so. She comes to the playground and is alarmed: the swings will surely harm the children, it cannot be right to shake their brains around so. She goes shopping with Antigona and enjoys the moving staircase. Antigona buys her a new funeral suit, and one for her dad, from Peacocks. Fatmire phones Blerta and gets her advice: Blerta is for Antigona, of course. And Fatmire makes up her mind.

While Antigona is at work, Fatmire leaves Afrim in bed and walks herself to the bus stop, gets on the correct bus with the correct money just as Antigona has shown her, gets off in Clissold Park, walks to Agim's house, and rings the doorbell. Only Era is there, with the children, but Fatmire insists that Era call Agim. He is cabbing that morning, and arrives fairly quickly. They all have coffee. Agim has a whisky. Fatmire makes her announcement: Antigona is to be asked to the wedding, or she, Fatmire, will not attend herself. Agim is overwhelmed, suddenly, by having his mother in his house, holding his children. He had thought she was dead. He starts to weep.

Imagine it, says Antigona, full of pride. Her mother,

negotiating London buses. Her mother, braving her brother for her sake.

'Fantastic,' I say. 'What a lady.' And it helps me, too, to see past Fatmire's impassive brown face to the active, loving mother of whom Antigona so often speaks.

And so Antigona does attend the wedding – in a shift dress from Wallis, in the end, looking like the ageing Christine Keeler in the photographs. Jennifer is billowing out of a shiny white dress; Hasan is too thin for his suit; Fatmire, Agim, Driton, and Afrim make up a dark back row, all red-eyed and sucking their teeth; Ylli, in a bow-tie, and Agim's daughters, in satin, burn across the front. Afterwards, released, they go back to Era's house and eat and drink. Agim informs Antigona in the kitchen that she is permitted in his house only while his mother is here: afterwards, conditions of excommunication will once more apply.

'What did you say then?'

'Just, you know, OK.' Antigona bites her lower lip. 'Just, you know, keep going.'

She makes a gesture of extending and balancing plates. 'Just give out the cake, for the party.'

It was Antigona who told me the beginning of the story of her father's white donkey, from her mother's point of view, full of practicality and dark humour. Soon after Afrim and Fatmire went home, Ylli told me the end of it, from his Grandad's point of view, as shouted to him from his Grandad's bed, from his Grandad's smoke-fug.

Fatmire had lent the donkey to Vera's husband in the autumn to carry wood back from the forest. It wasn't right. Afrim would never have lent the donkey – she was too old for such work. Vera's husband was a brute – all his own beasts were in a terrible state. Fatmire had always hated the donkey. And look what happened. The brute had overloaded the donkey, and the poor beast had missed its footing and fallen down a ravine where no one could reach her. No one told Afrim, or he would have gone down there somehow, shot her before she died that way, slowly, horribly, of a broken back. It was Fatmire's fault, all of it. She lent it to Vera's husband on purpose, and he overloaded it on purpose, and the donkey was too old, the donkey was just too old. Sometimes, you are just too old.

Ylli is nearly in tears over this story. He loves donkeys. 'Granny wouldn't do that,' he says to me, and I say of course not.

'Maybe the donkey just – had a heart attack, you know,' says Ylli, huskily. 'Maybe it was, like, an accident.'

'Oh, yes,' I say, 'I expect so. Nobody would want that to happen. Nobody would want it to work out that way.'

9
Who Do They Think They Are?

Quake Theory

> *When two plates of earth scrape along each other*
> *like a mother and daughter*
> *it is called a fault.*
>
> *Sharon Olds*

APRIL 2006

Flora and Antigona are staging one of their magnificent arguments in my kitchen. The subject is skirt lengths. Or it started off that way – we seem to be on the niqāb, now. Antigona is on my right, at the stove, boiling milk. She is wearing city shorts, heels, and a silk vest. Flora is on my left, sipping mango juice, swathed from head to foot in white cotton, like Audrey Hepburn in *A Nun's Story*. All at once, like an operatic chorus, they both turn to me for backup. I drop my head on the table, theatrically.

'I'm on both your sides,' I say. And, when they both laugh and shriek abuse at me:

'No. Really. I mean it.' I sit up, flushed, my head spinning. I realize I'm near to tears.

'You've got to let me. Please.'

OCTOBER 2004

Just three weeks after Antigona found her mother, she lost her younger daughter.

When Antigona went to wake Mihane for college that Tuesday morning, she found her room strangely quiet. When she lifted the duvet she found, curled on the pink sheet, the outsize stuffed dog Mihane had won at the fair. When she ran out to the stairwell, down the stairs, onto the street, she found nothing, there was nothing and nobody. She found herself unable to scream. When she called Mihane on her mobile phone, Mihane would not answer.

When Antigona went to Mihane's friend Laureen, whom she abominated, Laureen told her that Mihane had called and said she could never see Laureen again and she was sorry. When Laureen called Mihane on her mobile phone, Mihane would not answer. When Antigona went to the police, they told her they would not look for Mihane since they knew where she was: with Social Services. When she went to Social Services they told her that Mihane had put herself in their care and had been assigned a hostel place. They would not say where: Mihane was over sixteen and therefore Antigona, though her parent, was not entitled to the information. When Antigona begged them for a meeting, or a phone call, they refused. When she called Mihane on her mobile phone, Mihane would not answer.

When I called the mobile number, Mihane, surprisingly, picked up and we had a long conversation during which, between sobs, she begged me to tell her mum she loved her, she was OK, and she was not coming home. When Antigona called using my number, which of course she could not resist doing at once, Mihane put the phone down, and after that she must have sold her phone or lost it, because the number didn't ring any more, and we heard nothing from Mihane – bar a couple of phone-box calls to Ylli at New Year – for the next seven months, during which Antigona dreamed of her every night, spoke of her every hour, and suffered horribly.

How had this happened?

We had a lot of time to think about that. Nevertheless, it took a long time for the story to emerge: Antigona has no time for Freudian retrospect, and less for self-blame; Mihane is too careful and too loyal to tell me anything which would reflect badly on her mother; and it took me far too long to see the obvious.

When I was a schoolteacher, I used to tell my classes that a man driving into a tree and dying suddenly was not a tragedy; it was simply sad. A tragedy is what happens to someone heroic as a result of a human flaw in her character, I would say. A tragedy is grand and dramatic and also inevitable: you know it is going to happen, that's why you can't stop watching. In those terms, what happened to Antigona, Flora and Mihane is certainly a tragedy. All three of them are heroic in my eyes – stoical, ingenious, honest, loving, brave – but their circumstances were stacked against them like a mile of loose scree on an Albanian hillside. It only took one kicked pebble for the whole mountain to tumble on their heads.

Like everybody else, I used to think of Flora and Mihane together: a glossy-haired, bright-eyed, eager-to-please chorus. So much so, in fact, that I cannot remember for certain if it was Flora who negotiated the terms of her mother's job, or Mihane who walked round the house for the first time, asking if I expected to have ironing done; if it was Mihane I found operating the vacuum cleaner one afternoon when her mother was sick, or Flora bent over the bath with a scrub pad. I sent someone home. I wrote out a list of jobs and figures for the other, and she nodded.

When they were teenagers, I had their mobile numbers together in my book, under 'b' for babysitting. When I went to visit Antigona, they were all giggles, kholed brown eyes, matching Nike tracksuits, identical jeans. The last time I saw them together, they were arm in arm in the street, seventeen and fifteen, wearing sweatshirts which said *Gap* and *Gap*, waving to a four-year-old Sam through the basement window. He had laid a line of chairs across the sitting room, placed a bear on each cushion, clambered into the driver's seat, and was now steering his train triumphantly over imaginary mountains with bold turns of the colander. The girls' joy at this silk and plush, pink and gold vision of riches and security seemed, as ever, generous and entirely genuine.

'Chalk and cheese', one of their teachers said of them to Antigona, and she reported the phrase back to me for clarification. Actually, I think the teacher may simply have meant 'they don't get on'; for 'chalk and cheese', along with our other rural metaphors – chips off old blocks, opened floodgates, lonely furrows – is rather losing its meaning. Very few people now have made and seasoned a cheese, as Fatmire has, or sliced chalk from a quarry, as my great-grandfather did, and observed how precisely the one resembles the other and how the likeness only grows closer as they age and yellow and crumble, until you could only really distinguish between them by biting down and getting a mouthful of unyielding, filthy stone.

But the teacher's report was exact: appearances are deceptive and the girls are very different. Mihane, like her Aunt Blerta, is practical, capable and persistent, able to mend an electrical circuit and turn up at school regularly, able to get, hold, and be promoted in a Saturday job at M&S. She accumulates a neat stack of GCSEs, grades D–B, a bank account, and the universal mild approval of her teachers. Flora is volatile, brilliant and idle, capable of staying in bed for a week or writing an 'A' essay in an afternoon. She drives her teachers wild, except for those who adore her, and, according to her mother at least, has no concept of money. Mihane at fifteen will speak only English, even at home: Flora at eighteen floats between languages, fluent in six but unable to turn up for her 'AS' level Italian exam because she was depressed. Because Flora gets depressed. 'I remember,' she says. 'I remember where I came from. Everything that happened. All the time.' She gets ill, too, with troubles which all flare up from the torture-wound on her back: kidney infections, inflammation of the hip, something like rheumatism. Mihane, on the other hand, has her mother's extraordinary physical strength and air of deep-seated health. She says she never thinks about Kosovo. Never looks back. She gets on with the next thing.

She needs to: each day is full of its own troubles. The girls have been thrust, just on the cusp of adolescence, out of the age-old strictures and deep sexual taboos of the Kanun of Lek, into the vaunted, compulsory, debased sexuality of *Nuts* and Channel Five; out of a monoglot, clannish, absolutely homogenous society into the aggression and colour, the lurid, indecipherable mores of a racially mixed East London community school. What are they supposed to think? How are they supposed to behave? Each day they face this, this huge, impossible, lonely task.

It does not help that their mother is beginning to allow herself her own sexual appeal at exactly the moment when they are discovering theirs. It certainly does not help that their mother shares their clothes, fills out their jeans, and draws all the energy in a room to herself as soon as she enters it. It does not help, even, that they are so beautiful, that Mihane has a figure like Lara Croft and Flora hair and eyes like My Little Pony. People might think they are doing it on purpose. Albanian boys might point and stare, Jamaican boys might whistle through their teeth. See how the body catches you out? It can coat you in shame before you have even gone out in the morning. Skirt or trousers? Which length? How tight? Make-up? Flora is frequently defeated by the whole thing and stays in bed: Mihane settles for covering her racehorse legs in an oversized track suit and gets in on time.

Who can they look to? Their teachers are overstretched as it is, and their classes contain far more desperate cases than Antigona's daughters, who, by the standard of children of asylum-seekers in this country, are extraordinarily balanced, organized, and high-achieving. Antigona's blind faith and unrelenting demands on them as children have done that for them, but exactly what she wants of them as women, which is what they are becoming, is harder to discern. Not to marry like an Albanian, but not to have boyfriends like an English girl, either. To be flirtatious and admired at all times, but never to kiss anyone. To remember the shame of the Kanun and to forget it, at one and the same time. To be just like their mother, who is various as Cleopatra.

So, the girls need other role models, but it is difficult for them to mix. They are rarely allowed friends back to the house. Antigona and the uncles won't let them visit black or Turkish families, and the Pakistani community is very closed. There are a number of Kosovan and Albanian families in the area, but Antigona (and by extension her girls) is viewed as a dangerous person by many of the patresfamilias, so the girls are not taken into Albanian homes, cosseted and yelled at and urged to eat up, as they would sorely like to be.

They lack family. They miss their clan. Their uncles are frightening people for them, because of all the shamings and the rows. Flora, in particular, misses her father's relatives: the aunts and grandmother she loved and Antigona hated. The girls miss their father, for all his brutality. His fate is a source of guilt and misery for both of them: Mihane because she called the police, Flora because she was his last victim. The memories of his violence and his sporadic kindness fester unaired. Flora and Mihane went down to speak at his last deportation hearing and to say goodbye, but they are not permitted ever to mention this to their mother.

Though their mother is rarely there. For four years, from Mihane's twelfth to her sixteenth birthday, her mother works sixteen hours a day, six or seven days a week. She works to pay back their passage, she works to get them the luxuries she has dreamed of all her life, she works to build up a nest egg in case she is deported, she works because she is in the habit of labour, because this is the best chance she has ever had, she works to anaesthetize her memories of violence and terror and her gnawing grief for her lost family. All this Mihane understands: money worries her very much; she would never ask her mother to stop. Nor do she or Flora outwardly resent, as English girls might, being left alone to look after their little brother. 'It is our culture,' they tell me, proudly: in the Malësi, the older children look after the younger. When Antigona was Ylli's age, it was Blerta who fed and bathed and clothed her: Fatmire was working in the fields. The girls accept their duty, as they have all their lives. But in a Kosovan village they would have been in a group, surrounded by women of the *fis* doing similar jobs: here, they are alone, in the crucible of their very tidy maisonette, their small, assertively messy bedroom, enjoying what Antigona sees as unbelievable luxury and leisure. The girls are free, she tells me again and again, free from hunger and cold. They miss nothing. So night after night, the girls try on clothes, use the phone, watch the TV, and bicker: because, as they both tell me, actually, they are very different from each other. People tend to lump them together, but actually they're chalk and cheese. Actually, being different from each other is the business of their lives.

Women are very intolerant of each other's differences, I think. Especially if the other woman is close – a peer, a friend, a sister. I see it in the playground: mothers flinching and tutting at each other because one has returned to work and the other stayed at home, or even because both have returned to work but for different hours, because one has chosen a childminder and the other a nursery. I see it in my work: the hypercritical eye women writers turn on each other's creations, the rage of established women authors against young upstarts. I feel it rise up, thick and poisonous, in myself: against the mother who tells me *her* baby 'makes his own bedtime', against the sole woman writer on the platform – instead of against the men who put her there.

It is about representation, I think. I resent the woman on the platform because I fear she will be taken to represent all women writers and therefore me, and, in my eyes, is representing me wrongly. People will think I am like that, like that woman, they will think I am chalk when in fact I am cheese. The rage comes back to me about my poems: in public criticism I am accused of representing women – all women – too 'conservatively' or too 'radically'; in private I receive odd emails from women convinced a particular poem is about them. They are angry because, in representing what I thought was myself, I have represented them, wrongly.

This rage, like all the richest anger, comes from the most vulnerable parts of the self. If you are a woman, what people think of you is part of yourself. 'Men watch women, women watch themselves being watched,' as I have been repeating to myself ever since I read it in John Berger when I was twenty. Women make themselves up out of reflections, and they use other women as reflections. That is why women surround themselves with images of women, not men: women are mirrors, and the mirror is the self. Am I like that one? they say – or that one? Am I fatter than her? Sexier than her? Should she be ashamed? O mirror, does my bum look big this?

Flora and Mihane are in a subset of two: Albanian girls in London with a divorced mother. They have to represent each other. They are at the age when girls are at their most intolerant of their own reflections, when teenagers less solidly loved than Antigona's daughters starve themselves or slash open their arms. Every morning these two mirror each other, face to face in their matching, shared clothes.

Oddly enough, in this relationship, it is mercurial Flora who takes on the role of the puritan law-enforcer, rule-maker, voice of the Kanun; and the pragmatic Mihane who must therefore play the criminal. It is all those years as the older sister, partly: also Flora's experience of the Kanun was three years longer; also Flora's experience of chaos was even more painful than Mihane's, because she was tortured, so her need for order is stronger; also Flora is extremely clever and her sort of cleverness takes her to the word and the law. So Flora decides when they must come home from school, who Mihane can talk to while they are there, which characters on soap operas to approve or condemn. Mihane, at sixteen, says her youth worker, 'looks as if she would explode at any moment'.

This creates problems when Ahmed arrives on the scene. It is hard to maintain your stance on the moral high ground when you are the one with the hidden mobile phone and the secret assignations, and your sister is the one who has turned down twenty-six invitations from boys to the school prom and gone with her friends instead. And even harder to maintain a superior tone when you need your younger sister's collusion to have your boyfriend round in the evenings when your mother is working. But one of Ahmed's attractions for Flora is his religion. He is not leading Flora astray: he is leading her to the Koran. He is a bulwark against the chaos she sees all around her, not chaos itself. Mihane, meanwhile, seems attracted to the chaos. She may have no boyfriend, but she does have a tendency to make friends with loud, outgoing girls. With one in particular: Laureen.

Laureen is in Mihane's maths class. She is black, tall

and slim, giving Mihane a run for 'Best Bod of Year 10'. She has a bouncy walk and a loud voice and beaded cornrows and beautiful eyes and a huge, confident smile. She has loads of friends and gets it just right with boys: they all fancy her but none of them would talk dirty behind her back. She gets it just right in school, too: does exactly enough work to keep the teachers happy but not so much that anyone could call her a boff; gives Mr McClatchey a big cheeky smile when he tells her to be quiet, just to let him know who is in charge. She's got two voices: nice and clear for the teachers, deep down-homey for her friends. Laureen calls Mihane 'girlfriend', pretending they're in a movie. Laureen makes a space for her in her gang. She calls her 'Mish'.

'Black girl' was what little Mihane was always called back in Kosovo, because of her olive colouring, and it was always abusive, always in contrast to Flora's prized pale skin. Well, now she is a black girl, like Laureen, and it seems fine. Mihane and Flora have both learned the terms 'racist' and 'culture' and 'values' and 'prejudice' at school. Both of them use them fearlessly against any sort of discrimination against them, and both of them shout their mother down when she voices the crude racist prejudices of the Malësi. All the same, Mihane fears her mother's rage if she makes a black friend. Flora says she thinks Laureen is a bit loud, that she might not have such a good reputation, but Mihane knows her reputation is perfect. 'Come back to mine,' Laureen says. 'I'll cornrow your hair.'

So Mihane does. She trades days and evenings with

Laureen for Flora's days and evenings with Ahmed. Both of them forbid Ylli to tell, on pain of nameless torture. All that summer, the girls dump Ylli in the £1-a-day sport scheme and go back to their obsessions. Flora and Ahmed decide that such love has never been felt before and they must marry forthwith. Mihane falls in love with Laureen's extended Jamaican family, the brothers and sisters and nieces and nephews and grandmothers and aunts. It is noisy and busy and irregular: a permissive, dynamic version of an Albanian *fis*. And comforting, too – Laureen's churchgoing, teetotal, long-married parents are the very opposite of Antigona's dark fantasies of drug-taking orgiastic black families; Laureen's mother launches into high-decibel tirades against her children's late nights or slatternliness, and then calms down, just like home; Laureen, for all the mouthiness, is a youngest child, sheltered and supported and cherishing her cherry. Ahmed promises Flora that his mother back in Iraq will love her. If they can ever get there. But he's got family in Germany – they'll love her, too. They'll have a wedding here and a wedding in Germany and one in Iraq. Mihane and Laureen loll on the sofa, watching the TV, talking to Laureen's older brother, his flirty friends. They get similar GCSEs and decide together to do GNVQ Business at college. Ahmed says he doesn't mind about the headscarf – just so long as Flora covers herself properly. No white jeans! Flora adopts the dress-over-trousers look, which is rather in vogue. She has never been so happy. Mihane cornrows her hair and borrows Laureen's short shorts – just for inside the house! She looks *hot*. She learns to drawl. She changes her name to Mish. She has never been so happy. In August it is insanely hot and bright. Halcyon days.

Halcyon days, if you remember, end when the wrath of Zeus returns to smash the nest. In this case they end, for Mihane as well as Flora, when Agim comes round in his cab and catches Ahmed in the house. While Agim is chasing Ahmed and Flora round the estate, Mihane sneaks out to stay at Laureen's. Partly, she wants to escape what she knows will be a horrible scene, but mostly, so strongly has Flora impressed her with her own sinfulness, both for colluding with her and for taking up with Laureen, that she is afraid that she is next.

Early the next morning, Flora and Ahmed are married in the mosque. Later, she will buy a white wedding dress and the two will take pictures of each other in their bedsit, the perfect couple. Flora is sure she is in the right, and she is finding ever more comfort in Ahmed's talk of God's will. Meanwhile, Antigona calls Mihane and simply begs her to come home. Mihane comes, and the two are passionately reconciled. Antigona assures her again and again that she is her good girl, that she has always loved her just as much as Flora, that it is solely Flora's fault that she hasn't been giving Mihane so much attention in the last months. For a week or so, while Flora is in exile, Mihane warms herself in the sun of her mother's regard. And then Antigona goes off to Albania, and leaves Mihane alone with Ylli, and Mihane calls Laureen and asks her over.

*

But surprisingly quickly – a matter of days – after Antigona came back from Albania, she was reconciled with Flora. This was achieved by Flora patiently and persistently turning up at Antigona's house at around six in the evening, in the crucial interval between nannying and restaurant shifts, and taking loads of abuse. Flora's technique was simply to sit there until a pause came in the torrent of words, and then, swiftly, insert some item of gossip or a tale about a purchase, and before you knew it, Antigona would be condemning someone else or assuring Flora that her bargain wasn't nearly as good as the one Antigona had spotted in Wilkinson's. Antigona loves her elder daughter: she also likes her more than almost anyone in the world. Flora is so bright, so quick and so funny – together, Antigona and she can laugh at almost anything, including (which is disconcerting for outsiders) the things over which they most passionately disagree.

Flora developed a mania for cooking, and started to turn up earlier and earlier and make elaborate meals for the whole family. She did the ironing. She offered to sit with Ylli for the evening while Antigona was working. She did it again. Ahmed came round while Antigona was out and taught Ylli chess. Ahmed took Ylli out to play football after school. And Ahmed came round for dinner. I did not point out that this was the remedy I had suggested in the first place.

Me: So he's not such a monster after all?

Antigona: No. He is nice boy. He is soft – he do whatever she tell him. It's her I blame, actually. My daughter.

Me: For getting married?

Antigona: She has thrown away her future.

Me: She says she's still going to school.

Antigona: Now she has a husband she can't go to school! She have to work. She have to do whatever he tell her. All the cooking. The house.

I am about to say that Ahmed isn't an Albanian husband, and Flora isn't Antigona, and anyway, they don't have a house, but then I reflect that, in fact, Flora *is* behaving oddly. The cooking, for a start. The hours spent in her mother's house – she can't be going to school. And she has given up her receptionist job and gone to work in Miss Selfridge. The hours and pay are worse, but she prefers, she tells me, to work in an all-female environment. More modest. And she is studying Arabic, picking it up at the same frightening pace that she acquired English. She is reading the Koran. She raises her eyebrows when her mother goes to Tesco in a knee-length skirt. She says *she* wouldn't dress like that, now she is a married woman. She is trekking back to the moral high ground as fast as her new, ankle-concealing, boots will carry her. Why not? What exactly has she done except fall in love, get married and find God? She is whiter than white.

Mihane can't take it. Flora back at the centre of the home, sucking in her mother's scarce attention. All that Koran guff. She tells Laureen about it, goes out with her after college. They walk down the High Street together, arm in arm, then duck into an alley for a few puffs on a cigarette. Laureen has taken to this recently: Mihane doesn't like it much. Then Laureen has a text on her mobile: a cousin is round the corner, outside KFC. They go to meet him. He has a friend with him – tall and handsome. They eat chips and chat and pass another cigarette round. 'Hey,' says the friend to Mihane – he is quiet and graceful – and leans over suddenly and kisses her. At this exact moment Antigona passes by on her way to work.

So now it is Mihane who is taken home and shamed. A black guy! Black! In the street! Kissing! Mihane, like me, has learned to live with her mother's casual racism. Like me, she doesn't fully believe in it. Antigona's appalling and ludicrous racial stereotypes seem to belong to her Albanian self: to her crazy, antiquated past, to the Albanian language. In the Malësi, there are no black people, just an idea of them as a debased, bestial layer of humanity, a people lower even than the Roma. But, in the Malësi, an idea of Antigona the divorced woman also exists which Mihane well knows to be false. Here in England, in what Mihane thinks of as the real world, Antigona has surely put away those ideas. And here in England, many of the people Antigona likes best and who are most like her are black: her immediate neighbour; Ylli's Year 3 teacher; the woman at the Council she always waits to see in preference to the other clerks; Tony, for heaven's sake, the nearest she has ever come to a boyfriend.

But now all the terrible names are coming out, the Albanian words that Mihane has refused to translate into English, even in her head. Mihane squats on the floor, hands over her head, and works on not translating them, the words for monkey, slave, horned monster, ape, dog, bitch, bull, cow, pizzle. Blows strike her clasped hands. The Kanun of Lek has overtaken her lovely, laughing mother. The Kanun is clear, it is black and white, and Mihane is black, sexually and racially black; her blood, inherited directly from her father, is all black.

The blows stop. They were mostly symbolic – there will be no bruises.

'I won't do it again,' Mihane says, as she did when she was a child. 'I won't, Mummy, I promise.'

Antigona sags exhausted into a chair. Mihane crawls off into her room, puts her headphones on. Flora comes in, sets about the supper. Under the duvet, Mihane reaches for her mobile phone, sends a text to Laureen. CU tomorrow xxxx. She thinks about the cousin's friend. She wishes she had a cigarette.

Antigona isn't in a good way, actually. The euphoria of finding her family has faded, and bubbling up in her, though she will not pause to diagnose it, is the grief and fear and mourning for them she has been repressing for six years. She is extremely worried about the money she has just sent to Jehona. Of course, she must save her sister's life – but the £10,000 was her security, very painfully won. Her brothers' blamc and ostracism on top of this hurts her intolerably. It leaves her bewildered, furious, horribly lonely.

Finding her family has reunited Antigona with her Albanian self: with her mother's love but also with the Kanun and all her internalized shame. She doesn't know quite where she is any more: when she speaks on the phone to her sister and then looks up to see a wall of flats, a multicultural Hackney bus, she feels her old and new selves collide. She is working longer hours than ever, partly to spite Agim, partly to get away from her house, mostly to earn money to make up for what she has given away to Jehona, and the exhaustion is catching up with her. She has quarrelled bitterly with a girl at work over a share of the tips. She is enraged with both her daughters. Her eyes are glassy and her skin has a stretched, yellow look. Anyone could see, looking at her, that here was a woman on edge; here was a firecracker waiting for a match.

Now, there was an Albanian girl who lived on her own in the opposite block to Antigona. She was a very bad girl; on this Flora and Antigona agreed. She was abandoned by her family, she took drugs, she was a prostitute. I don't know if more than the first was true: I do know that this girl, whom they talked of often, on whom they liked to agree, represented their worst fears. She was the bottom of the heap, she was Chaos, she was What Might Happen. And this girl, just a couple of days after the kiss, came up to Flora as she was walking to her mother's house, and told her that Mihane was in there with some black guys, smoking drugs. Mihane, she repeated, was smoking drugs in the street and having sex with black guys. Flora was horrified, terrified, the street opened up in front of her: without pausing to consider why the girl might be telling her this, or where she got her information from, she called her mother and summoned her back from the restaurant.

Something happened, then, that night, in the flat. Mihane won't talk about it, except to say that she never took more than a puff or two of cannabis in her entire life, and that she never did more than kiss any guy. Antigona says mothers need to slap children, sometimes, for discipline. 'My mother always slap me,' says Antigona. 'It make me strong.' Antigona has seen so much violence in her life, she has suffered so many blows.

Something happened: it is three years now, and Mihane has never come back to her mother's house, she has never let her mother know where she lives. Something happened: Mihane is a good girl and loves her mother terribly. The day the girl in the flat below started screaming because her mother was beating her, Antigona had been a vigilante against violence. But that day, the day the Bad Girl accosted Flora, Antigona was not herself, she wasn't right. When women become mothers they do things they never believed possible: like pulling their child out of a fire, out of the sea, out of a country – and, sometimes, other things. Something happened: when Mihane went to the police, she asked to be taken into care because she was abused, because she was a victim of violence, and they believed her at once, so I think the Something must have shown on her face.

And just three weeks after *that*, unbelievably, Flora and Ahmed moved in with Antigona. She even bought them a nice new bed – not the intricately carved bed-and-chest set with which newlyweds are traditionally presented in the Malësi, but a double bed nonetheless, with a pocket-sprung mattress, lightly worn. The reasons were partly practical: Antigona needed someone to sit with Ylli while she was at work, and Flora volunteered night after night. Of course Ahmed came too, and soon they started staying over on late nights. From there, it was one short step – Ahmed losing his job – to their complete acceptance.

Antigona needs company. Mihane is utterly lost, and the wound is deep and raw. Her brothers – even Driton – have shut down all communication since Mihane's disappearance. This will be the Christmas of waiting for Mihane to call Ylli, of keeping the little mobile she gave him charged at all times, warm as an egg. This will be the New Year Antigona will leave boxes of dresses and pink high heels for her little nieces on Agim's doorstep, and he, in response, will bring his taxi to their flats, call Ylli down the stairs to the communal door, and, as Antigona watches over the balcony, count five ten-pound notes into the little boy's hand, turn him round and then send him back upstairs without saying a word.

Antigona needs someone in her house, even if that means leaving Flora and Ahmed in all day with the heating on, watching Al Jazeera and weird Koranic TV. Even if their obsessive sexual jealousy is proving more than an adolescent phase, and Flora tracks Ahmed everywhere he goes, on foot or by phone, to check he is not talking to any girls, and if he does – to the checkout girl in Tesco, for instance – stages seismic hysterical rows in front of Ylli. Even if Antigona is daily more certain that Flora has given up her studies, that Ahmed is too involved in his Islamic reading to have any real intention of finding another job.

In February, a letter for Antigona arrives from Mihane's bank. It is sent in error, in fact: Mihane started the account as a juvenile, with Antigona as a referee, and the bank has failed to notice Mihane's date of birth when sending out the letter. The account is being closed without notice because of 'irregularities'. The irregularity is very easy to spot: a cheque for £10,000 paid into the account one day and twenty withdrawals of £500 made in twenty different cash and pawn shops in central London the next, rapidly followed by the voiding of the original cheque. A petty fraud, the kind that could only succeed with collusion from a bank clerk, as the cheque and withdrawals went through none of the ordinary clearances. Antigona is utterly horrified. She thinks her daughter has become a major criminal. She is certain her daughter is a drug addict. I think her daughter may merely have had her cheque-book stolen. Antigona says, in that case, she would have reported it and the bank wouldn't be closing her account. I have to admit she has a point. We sit, pale and sick, contemplating Mihane in the 'heroin screws you up' advert; Mihane, purple and dead in a bedsit.

'They'd tell you if she were dead, you know,' I say, because Antigona is sobbing.

'Maybe not,' she says. 'These people, they think they know my child better than me. But no one love her better than me, no one know her better.'

I think about the boat, the fire, Mihane walking through the forest with Ylli on her back. Lately, Antigona has been full of stories of Mihane's babyhood and early childhood, how Antigona had to go back to the fields the day after she gave birth, how she worked with the baby tied always to her body, slept with her in her bed, and how good the little one was, how strong and calm. Here in England, I think, she worked on as if Mihane were still on her back – it did not occur to her to think such a bond could be broken or even needed to be voiced.

To distract Antigona, I start poring over the rest of the statement. Prior to the £10,000, all the payments and withdrawals are tiny – £43 credit each week from Social Services, £10 debits from cashpoints. From one particular cashpoint, a Link machine in a pub with a postcode. We ring up BT to decode the postcode. Croydon. Mihane is living in Croydon, how fantastically banal. I go to W.H. Smith and buy an A–Z. We find the street of the postcode, and that very weekend Antigona sets off to find her daughter. This is no small undertaking: Antigona's knowledge of Hackney side streets and shops is much better than mine, but she has very rarely ventured into central London, and hasn't negotiated a train station since her visit to Lunar House. But she is determined. She is convinced she will find Mihane. She has a fantasy of bringing her home and locking her up for weeks until she is free of drugs and evil influences. Or sending her to Albania, maybe, to teach her a lesson.

Antigona returns depressed. She has sat in the pub

for many hours sipping ginger ale and seen many young people – mostly black, she says, with a curl of her lip – and spoken to a number of them and shown them Mihane's photo, but no one registered even a flicker of recognition.

The next week, she returns and this time goes to the Croydon police, and instead of the serious sympathy she is used to, she finds herself blanked as soon as Mihane's name is put through the computer. 'Nothing we can do for you, madam,' they say, looking at her coldly. 'It's a Social Services matter.' The bank statement is burning a hole in her pocket: she thinks of showing it to them, having Mihane locked up, but when she comes to the counter no one pays her any attention and she turns for the long journey home.

Every day, Antigona bemoans her daughters, first to her mother on the phone, then to me. Flora has sunk into depression. She has given up school, she has given up work, she spends all day watching Koranic videos and phoning up Ahmed to check he really is at the mosque or the pool hall, as he says. In February, she finds he has gone to a cafe instead of the mosque and has a species of fit and goes blue and Ylli has to call an ambulance.

How can her girls have had all the choices in the world, says Antigona, every choice she, Antigona, was denied, and yet chosen to do this? Chosen to run away, to be a thief, a drug addict? Every day, every day she sees a girl who looks like Mihane in the street, every night she dreams of her. Or chosen to be Muslim, to marry at seventeen, to spend every day chasing after your husband – what life is that?

I say that it is very difficult to make choices to live differently from the way you were brought up. The way the daughters of alcoholics seek out another alcoholic to marry – *They are stupid,* spits Antigona. Yes, I say, but honestly they can't help it, any more than I, the daughter of a mild-mannered academic, could help marrying another mild-mannered academic – it makes us feel at home. Flora, I say, with her obsession with shame and the law, is making herself a little Malësi in her own house, constructing herself a little village. In her rage against the passive Ahmed, she is reproducing what she knows, making what she understands to be a marriage. And . . .

'I make my life different,' says Antigona. 'I changed.'

'You're exceptional,' I say, and it is true. But it doesn't necessarily help a daughter to have an exceptional mother. When it comes to self-determination, it can even make things worse.

'My girls take nothing from me.'

'I don't know. Whatever Mihane is up to, she's not exactly being weak-minded. Staying away this long – never calling, nothing – it's incredible.'

'She is stupid,' says Antigona. 'It is her father's blood.'

'No! Come on. Completely bloody-minded – doing everything for herself, never giving up – who does that remind you of? '

Antigona manages a smile. But in fact I am getting pretty worried about Mihane myself. I don't understand how she can be keeping this up without help, and I can't imagine what good person would want to help her. It is March now, a cold slow March, nearly six months since Mihane left, and nothing has shifted, any more than the shivering trees in London Fields have begun to bud.

But spring will come, with its intrusive new leaves, its fingers of new-angled light, even behind the shut curtains of a maisonette in Hackney. In April, Flora stirs herself, and goes to Brick Lane with her new Turkish friend Ayesha. She comes back with a whole new outfit. Hijab – and not just several headscarves, but a number of flowing burka-like garments which cover her shoulder to ankle. In a private ceremony with Ahmed, she puts on the whole kit, and vows never to take it off.

Antigona is hysterical with rage, as of course must have been part of the intention. Flora, she declares, looks old and ugly and like a Pakistani. She doesn't look like Antigona's daughter: she looks like her mother! What does she want to do that for? I make some liberal snufflings about women feeling free in the veil and liberating themselves from being sexual all the time, and Faith . . . But I am never very convincing on Faith, as I have none, and nor does Antigona. Life is for the living and the grabbing and then you die: one of the bedrock convictions Antigona and I have in common.

I realize Antigona is staring at me. 'Kate,' she says.

'When you see a woman wearing the sack thingy – up to the eyes.'

'The niqāb.'

'Whatever. Don't you think – you look stupid, take it off?'

I do, actually. Or that is one of my thoughts, but I fear it may be based in prejudice. Certainly, I find it very hard to imagine how a niqāb can be liberating. I heard a woman on the radio once, making an excellent case for liberation under the hijab, but when she got to explaining her own niqāb, she said it was needed for women and not for men because 'women are the candle and men are the moths', which seemed to me a dismal and reductive sexualization of everything rather than the reverse.

And it made me think – now, what is that little voice from deep inside me? Good Heavens, it's speaking Scots. I didn't know my subconscious could even do that any more. But here it is, saying quite clearly and rather sourly, 'Whaur d'ye think ye ere? The Queen o' Sheba?' In English: Just how sexy do you think you are, honey? I certainly do not intend to let this voice have any conversation with Antigona. They would get on all too well. Instead, I say how I regret the recent disappearance of Amanni's mum under the niqāb. Amanni is a lively little girl who always does up Sam's shoe straps at school, and I used to greet her mother on the street, but it is hard to say 'hello' to a beige veil, or believe it wants to talk to you.

Clearly, I need to speak to Flora about it. A DSS form arrives around this time, as Flora has been struck off her school roll and needs to declare herself either working or unemployed. As Antigona is absolutely not speaking to Flora, and as I am in any case always in charge of all official communication, I go off with the form to beard Flora in Miss Selfridge.

I have to admit it's a striking look. With her tiny, bony, slightly bent figure draped in black to her ankles, Flora from behind looks like a little old lady, of the kind that gathered round the guillotine. From the front, without her fairy-tale cloak of hair, Flora's features are suddenly large and stern. She looks punky, defiant as if she'd pierced her nose.

No lip-glossed smiles for me today. No lip-gloss, either – I imagine she has given it up. She suspects I'm after information for one of my newspaper articles and she is not willing to tell me, an infidel, why she has taken this step. 'It doesn't say you have to in the Koran, you know,' I say, having read the relevant verse that morning. 'The Koran just says you shouldn't dress more immodestly than is usual. Women and men.'

'That,' says Flora the lawyer, 'depends on what you think is usual.'

'What do they think here?' I say, indicating the racks of short tight clothes all around us, the dolled-up assistants. 'Don't you have to wear their clothes?'

'I am wearing their clothes,' she says, 'underneath. And they know the law.'

I note, however, that she seems to be mostly on rail-tidying duty. I produce my form and Flora signs it with airy, render-unto-Caesar disdain. 'I am happy to pay tax,' she says.

I point out she pays tax already, and is more likely to get credits now, and she shrugs. 'Will you work more hours?' I ask.

'No, I have so much to do in the house,' she says. 'For my husband.'

'Do you go to the mosque?' I ask.

'Oh, no,' she says. 'I study at home. But I know the Koran!'

'Your mother doesn't understand.'

'No, but I understand her. I always understand my mum, even when she doesn't understand me.' And she smiles, full of kindly enlightenment.

You have indeed, I consider, outmanoeuvred your mother, O Flora the lawyer manqué. Leaving aside your faith, which I will never understand, I must congratulate you on your ingenuity. The veil is the perfect answer to the conundrum your mother set you: how to be sexy and yet without shame, English and yet a proud daughter of the Malësi, how to grow up and be different from your mother. Under your drapes you are a Miss Selfridge babe, under your veil is your store of wayward hair, but all of this is hidden, kept for your husband, and your veil implies it, quietly, sexily, like the neat dark cover of a plush-lined jewel box. The hijab asserts your difference, but asserts your righteousness too. Antigona rages because she says you look oppressed, as if you have thrown away your life for a man, but she is wrong. This is a very powerful way to dress, particularly for its effect on other women. Shame on you, it says, and all around you women cede space. Shame on me. I step out of the shop, abashed.

Mihane calls. 14 May, ten in the morning, in my house on Antigona's mobile. Antigona is scarlet, eyes streaming, gesturing for me to take over the buttoning of the toddler, her whole body tense and thrust upwards, as if she were having difficulty staying on the ground. She is listening intently to something – a series of instructions – then breaks into 'Why won't you let me help you, Mihane?' in a voice so utterly desolate, so full of desperate love that I cannot imagine anyone resisting it.

And apparently Mihane can't, for, in another moment, Antigona has dived for her purse and is giving her name and debit card number in the cut-glass manner she has learned from me. '473. Yes. That is correct. Thank you. Could you hand the phone back to my daughter, please,' and the official does so, and Antigona's English promptly goes to pieces. Mihane is clearly not letting her speak Albanian. 'I love you,' she keeps saying, 'I love you, please. Your number, please.'

It was a gas bill, it turns out. Just fifty quid. An odd thing to have broken a runaway – but Mihane, I remember, was always worried about money, getting things paid on time, officials. When I made her mother go legal she wept because of the lost income, then wept again at the risks they'd been taking. It was one of the reasons I could never picture her as a bank robber.

She hasn't given her mother her number, though. 'But she will call me,' says Antigona, 'she will.' She looks suddenly younger, the way she did when she first found her family, as if her heart were beating properly again, as if blood were flushing all her veins.

And Mihane does call again, and again, and runs out of credit and gives her mother a number to call her back, which Antigona, with superb self-control, manages to do in moderation, just once a day. Mihane is working in a cafe, she reports, and living 'with some ladies'. She won't say more. She has explained about the bank. She was so stupid. Some boys wanted to borrow her chequebook. They said they'd give her £500 and no one would know, but they didn't give her anything and she had to beg the bank not to prosecute her and now she can't have an account any more. She has a boyfriend, Antigona thinks. Mihane says they can meet soon, but she keeps putting it off. She is ill, she says, sick.

At last, in late June, Mihane sets a date and a place. Saturday afternoon, under the Millennium Wheel. Flora goes too, and Ylli. Antigona returns resplendent, in new clothes. They have all been to H&M. She kitted Mihane out from top to toe; she spent £200! Of course, her clothes were nothing, she had nothing, but she looked pretty, so pretty! I think of holding my babies, their soft hair and warm heads, the intense physical experience that is missing them. Antigona has been holding her baby, and she is filled with happiness. Maybe Mihane will come to Albania with her – she is off in just three weeks – maybe the visa would be too difficult. Surely Mihane will come home soon. She is thin but so pretty, and her hair is highlighted – see!

I look at the photos – the three women peering into the light, their backs to the rail that runs by the river walkway. They look as if they were on a ship: the cruise Antigona sometimes fantasizes about. They might just have met: Mihane the leggy, dressed-down blonde in a cropped white T-shirt and tight jeans; Flora in one of her sternest burkas, her hijab a stark black and white, Antigona with her lush dark bob, showing her rounded arms and legs in a pretty amber frock. No one will ever confuse them again: they barely seem related.

'What do they want to do that for?' says Ahmed when the bombs go off in London on 7 July. Bombs, he says, are un-Islamic.

The bombs stop Antigona from seeing Mihane the weekend before she goes off for her four-week holiday in Albania. First they are both too scared to travel, then Mihane says she is sick. Never mind – when Antigona gets home . . .

Ahmed, meantime – responsible, even-tempered, hard-working Ahmed, with his curly dark hair and swarthy skin, and, recently, his round white hat – finds his life comprehensively ruined. He seems to be unemployable. He can clear a bus merely by getting on and opening his sandwich bag.

September. Antigona is back from Albania, tanned, confident, wonderfully empowered after four weeks playing the rich western auntie to her Albanian family. Mihane is still sick. Ahmed and Flora have spent the summer inside, it seems, fighting, and now Flora is intent on picking a fight with her mother.

'Flora,' says Antigona, 'says the bomb thingy – New York, the towers . . .'

'September 11th?'

'Yeah. She says, that was Jews. That is stupid, no?'

'Definitely stupid. Very stupid.' I read her a *Guardian* article, conveniently published that day on the very subject. She listens intently.

'Why do they want to believe those things?'

'Who – the journalists?'

'No! Flora and Ahmed. This is a conspiracy, this is the Jews . . .'

'Well,' I say, 'Ahmed's life here – it's pretty shit, right?'

'He should get a job.'

'He can't get a job! He looks like a terrorist.'

'He should take his hat off.'

'He'd just look like a terrorist with his hat off.'

'He should go back home, then. Let my daughter have her life.'

'Antigona, he comes from Iraq!'

'He say Germany.'

'Whatever. He can't go back there, and he can't get on here either. I think, the way he looks at it, the white guys are in charge in his country, and they're in charge here, and anyone who looks at him runs away and the only way he can find any dignity in himself is to go to the mosque and believe in all that stuff.'

'But it is stupid.'

'Yes. Well, not all of it.'

'Putting the scarf on! Jews do September eleven! This is stupid stuff. My daughter forgets. She forget how she come to this country, what is the life there! If the Americans do not come to save us, we would be dead. The Serbs came to kill us in our house. I do not forget.'

Mihane is lost again. Over the summer, she has changed her mobile phone, and hasn't told Antigona the new number. There was a call before she went to Albania, one when she came back – and now, nothing.

The months go by. Antigona misses her more, not less. Her anxieties, too, are redoubled. What could be keeping her, now? Who could be keeping her? What did they mean, the thinness, the sickness, the blonde highlights? Could she be a drug addict, a prostitute? It is the winter Jehona returns to her mother's house with the giant baby. Antigona talks to Fatmire every day, heavy talk, full of anxiety and shame.

Flora, meanwhile, has started a college course. Practical, this time: she is training to be a legal secretary. She comes round to tart up her CV and update me on her life. Of her marriage she says, 'I have a problem with jealousy. I can't work out whether it is because of my upbringing or actually because of something he is doing.' I look at her poised over the keys, her neat, black-and-white-wrapped head held up, her liquid eyes fixed at some ambitious point in the middle distance: like a little hunting creature, one paw curved and paused, scenting the wind.

'You're back,' I say, impulsively, the way I talk to her mum.

'I am,' she says, catching my meaning, as her mother often does.

Flora returns to her typing. Suddenly I look at her headscarf differently. I think it might be holding her together.

'She will never finish that course,' says Antigona sourly. 'She let everything go. It is because of him.'

'Oh,' I say, 'give her a break. She's a clever girl.' And I nip out before I have to listen to a diatribe about how Flora is letting herself, her brains and her mother down.

In November, Ahmed and Flora have a particularly enormous row, and Ahmed leaves to spend the night with a friend. Antigona, flushed with excitement, calls a conference, and tells Ahmed and Flora they are both young people, there is no shame in splitting up, and to get out of her house. Ahmed says he has left already, and taken a room. And that he *has* got a job, as a matter of fact, shifting pallets in a warehouse. And that his papers have finally come through. He will be an EU citizen, and will marry Flora in the register office. Antigona, who is always hoping for Ahmed to be spirited away in the night by Officials, is deeply disappointed, but not as disappointed as when Flora moves to join him the next night.

Then a pause. 'It's never dull at your house,' I like to joke with Antigona, but now it is. She gives up the restaurant to stay home with Ylli, and though the extra sleep clearly benefits her, the extra time to think drives her crazy. Where is Mihane? Who is holding her? When will they let her go?

A box for Albania, for the New Year. Mersela gets half a rack of Miss Selfridge clothes, many with the labels on, which Flora has bought but now deems indecent. Antigona has already picked out the shortest and most clingy garments for herself and makes a point of wearing them in front of Flora as often as possible. Mersela gets three of Mihane's tracksuits, left hanging in her wardrobe when she ran away. And, at the last minute, Mersela gets the fur-collared, wasp-waisted, quilted gold coat from New Look which Antigona had picked out for Mihane's Christmas present. It raises her status with her Tirana room-mates considerably and she never, never lets them borrow it.

Four days into the New Year, Agim is deported. It happens as suddenly as a joke: as if he, the fat guy with the moustache, had stepped on a trapdoor in a black-and-white film. On New Year's Day, he is outside his sister's door, refusing to come in, stout and judgemental as ever. The day his daughters resume school, he is in Pristina, a city he has never, in fact, previously visited.

The injustice, as well as the rigour, takes my breath away. Antigona sits in my kitchen for days, listing Albanians with criminal records and years of sponging off the Social Security behind them who yet, somehow, have amnesty and Indefinite Leave to Remain and the promise of citizenship. Agim, as she says over and over, is a refugee, a victim of torture, and a fanatical taxpayer. He should have the taxes back, she says. We owe him.

The deportation is like a death, or a murder: other concerns are forgotten in its wake. Antigona goes to Clissold Park every night, to help. Era and the girls are not deported, as their cases are still in process, and their solicitor advises them to stay put. He thinks they have a good chance of getting citizenship, and of passing citizenship in turn back to Agim. But Agim, his calls rattling all the phones on the table, is having none of it. A week after his departure, a long-held plan is put into action. Driton packs Agim's family, the mustard sofas, the heart-shaped cushions, and all their other worldly goods into a van he has bought for the purpose, and drives them across Europe to a new country – not Albania – a contact, and a job. On his return, Driton is on fair terms with his sister, but neither of them really has time to test their new relationship before another disaster strikes.

Antigona is always telling me her dreams, and I am always being dry about them.

'I dreamed Mihane, she was falling off a boat,' she says, and I tell her that dreams are a bodily process, random electricity in the brain to which she later attaches narratives.

'I dreamed Flora, she was being buried in a hole,' and I say that she must have been thinking about Flora just before she went to sleep, and that Flora is not in a hole, anyway, she has just passed Level 2 of her course.

'I dreamed Sam, he was holding a snake.' And I ask

her to please stop, because I can't be doing with spirits and interpretations. It reminds me too much of Victorian jokes about servants, their heads in a dream book.

But now it is March again, nine months since we last saw Mihane, eighteen months since she left, and Antigona has a dream about her. It is rather an unspecific dream, by Antigona's standards – Mihane is ill in bed, and Antigona can't get to her – but it recurs. The dream visits every night for seven nights, and then Antigona makes up her mind. On Saturday, she gets on the train and goes to Croydon to sit in the dismal postcode pub, and beg anyone who passes to tell her if they have seen the girl in the picture, her daughter Mihane.

Antigona isn't answering her phone on Sunday. I assume she has found nothing, and has taken herself shopping for consolation. Sure enough, she is pale and silent on Monday.

'You didn't find her, then?'

'No, I found her.'

'You found her? How? Tell me!'

Antigona sits down at the table and talks to her hands. The baby is wailing and I drag her onto my lap. Antigona went to the pub. She sat there for hours, asked everyone. Then an older guy came in with his teenage daughter – he was using the cash machine, just like Mihane. She went up to him, showed him the photo, and, just as he was shaking his head sadly, the teenager peered over his shoulder, and said that was Mish, you know, Anna's friend, Mish, who just had the baby.

A baby! Tears rush up my nose like champagne. Why hadn't I thought of it? Bizarrely, I behave like a Sloane at a wedding.

'Oh!' I say, 'Oh, darling, a baby, how wonderful!' And I hug Antigona's bony shoulders.

Silence.

'I knew it,' says Antigona.

'No, you didn't,' I say. 'You thought she was a prostitute and taking drugs. This is much better.'

'She is seventeen.'

'I know, but you can help her. You were seventeen!'

In my mind, Mihane is already installed in Antigona's cosy maisonette. The baby is coming to work with Antigona, Mihane is a model teenage mum, training to be . . . a nurse, that's it, and . . .

'I was married.'

'Is Mihane still with the boyfriend?'

Antigona shrugs.

'She won't talk about it?'

'I haven't spoken to her.'

'Haven't you got her number – did the girl have her address?'

'No – I've got her number. The dad, he made her give it to me.'

'But you haven't called her?'

'No.'

'But—'

'That is a bastard child.' Antigona slumps.

'Yeah – but no one cares about that here.'

'The problem is – what sort of baby.'

'Well, a baby – do you mean, boy or girl?'

'No. What *kind* of baby.'

I don't understand. I don't get it at all. I bring the phone.

'You need to ring her,' I say. And Antigona does ring, her face white with two scarlet spots under the eyes, her mouth thinned till it has almost disappeared. The mask face, I recognize too late, the Fury face, the face of the Kanun of Lek.

'You see,' the Kanun's joyless flat voice says to Antigona's darling daughter, 'I can find you anywhere.' Then, 'How old is he, the baby?' then 'What colour is he? What colour is the baby?' and I realize what this is all about.

This is the first open argument Antigona and I have ever had. Or rather, I have never before fought all of Antigona, only one part of her – usually the Albanian bit – while cheerleading her more liberal instincts. She proves an appalling and terrifying opponent. Appalling and terrifying things – awful, implausible, melodramatic dialogue, says my inner radio dramatist – are being said in my house, on the hour, by the hour, over the lovely downy head of my baby, whose blondness I now wish Antigona would stop admiring.

'I won't accept it.'

'You can't not accept it. The child is there. It's not asking you for permission to live.'

'I'll just go on with my life and she has her life, that's it.'

'You'll still have a grandchild.'

'That is not my grandchild.'

'That's your daughter. That's your grandchild.'

Antigona hisses as she clips up the pushchair: 'That is not my grandchild. My blood is white.'

I shout down the garden, 'Your blood is red, and the baby's blood is red.'

I have often asked myself, how prejudiced am I, really? Like every other middle-class person I know, I am, in theory, passionately anti-racist. As a student, I was actively anti-apartheid. As a teacher, which I was for ten years, I constantly taught relevant texts and debated the subject, often with apparently racist students. But I am also aware that, like most middle-class people, I live in a largely white world. I have very little contact with my Pakistani and Turkish neighbours; my son goes to a school where twenty-seven languages are spoken, but only English was used at his birthday party.

But now, now, I am up against racism that can make a woman hate her daughter and deny her own flesh, and I find I hate it, all right. It would be reassuring, if it weren't so painful to hate someone you love. Should I fire Antigona? I am finding it unbearable to be near her. I find myself focusing on her hands: the strong, knuckly, unbeautiful hands that she showed me when we first met, the hands that have done so many kind things for me and my children, which clasp round my baby's round tummy, comb her soft hair into a clip. Hands that want to push away her daughter, that refuse to hold her daughter's child. Listen, she is off again: the adoption fantasy. Listen how feeble I am.

'She can give away the child and come back here

and start again. I do not mind! Then the child have his life and she have her life, and later, when the child is twenty, she can meet again.'

'Does Mihane say she wants to have the child adopted?'

'No! But she is stupid.'

'Would you have given away Flora when you were seventeen?'

'No, but I was married.'

'Well, I don't think Mihane will give away her baby. That's not how she was brought up.'

I think about Mihane, seventeen, with a battered, leaking body and a six-week-old baby. I ask Antigona for her number, which she gives me readily, because, despite my sincere and constant protestations to the contrary, she still believes that I am her friend and therefore on her side. Perhaps she thinks I am going to shame Mihane.

'Hiya.' I am startled. Mihane, or rather Mish, sounds like a black girl from Croydon. Her accent is so thick, I actually find her a little hard to understand. There is a TV on in the background, a baby snuffling.

She is easy to talk to, as she always was, soft, grateful, puzzled. I ask her about the birth, which was painful and left her pelvis twisted, the baby, who is big and whom she is breastfeeding. I ask about how she is living, and she explains, with the baby's grandmother. Ah. Mihane has pitched up in an extended Jamaican family with traditional, churchgoing parents and rather wilder children, just like Laureen's. The relationship with the boy is over, but his mother has taken her in, made her at home, stayed with her through the birth, and is helping her with everything. I know this will be stones to Antigona, I know she will never bring herself to acknowledge this black mirror image of herself.

'It's just like home, really,' says Mihane, 'the family. Grandmas and everything. Mum would like them.'

I tell Mihane what I will say over and over in many phone calls, tell her the things she needs to hear from somebody near her mother, even me: that she is in the right and her mother in the wrong. That her baby is a lovely baby. That she is a good, brave girl and doing so well. I tell her about how she herself was born, how her mother returned to the fields with her on her back the next day, and she cries. I tell her all the stories her mother has told me, about the stoical little girl her mother relied on so much, and I go back and tell Antigona about the brave young mother I have been speaking to.

'Maybe the baby won't look so black,' says Antigona. 'Maybe – half-caste – you can't always tell?' And maybe I should jump down her throat right then, maybe I should launch another onslaught on her attitudes and language, but I don't – I sit on my hands. And Antigona, while not for a moment ceding an inch of moral high ground, starts to make arrangements to get to Croydon, to meet Mihane in the shopping centre by the station—

Which is when, with the most melodramatic timing possible, her lawyer calls. Something has gone wrong with her application for more Leave to Remain. Something happened when Agim left. An irregularity was unexpectedly discovered.

10

Your Nanny, Your Mum

She was a battered woman now, not a lovely girl; but she still had that something which fires the imagination, could still stop one's breath for a moment by a look or gesture that somehow revealed the meaning in common things. She had only to stand in the orchard, to put her hand on a little crab tree and look up at the apples, to make you feel the goodness of planting and tending and harvesting at last. All the strong things of her heart came out in her body that had been so tireless in serving generous emotions.

It was no wonder that her sons stood tall and straight.

Willa Cather, *My Antonia*

'Kate,' says Ylli, 'do you mind if I ride along there?'

I stop. He is pointing to a section of block edging which has come adrift from the compacted mud of the towpath and now forms a sort of catwalk, three inches wide, curving over the greenish murk of the canal. Sam has already braked his little bike and is leaning, rapt, on his handlebars. Every outing with Ylli yields at least one such show.

'All right,' I say. 'But if you fall in you'll have to get yourself out. And Sam – don't even think about it.'

Ylli is off. A long run-up, then he whirls out on his death-defying tour and is back on the towpath, doing a wheelie, no hands, laughing, before we can blink.

'Can I do it again?'

'Only if you don't mind being late for the first session.'

We're off again. Skating: it's our new thing. For a couple of years, it was swimming. We went every day for a whole half-term, once: me, frozen to the marrow in the deep end while Ylli taught the improbably tiny Sam to do pencil jumps and to swim down twelve feet to pick up my goggles. Ylli himself had been taught to swim by the school at the age of seven, or, rather: 'When we got there, they divided us up into people that could swim and people that couldn't swim, right, and if you could swim you got in the big pool and swam across it, and I wasn't going in the baby pool, right, so I just jumped in the big pool and invented how to swim and I did it! They put me in the good group.' Actually, I don't think they taught him much. Ylli swims with the stroke of boys in rivers everywhere: arm over arm, head up, muscles flashing like dolphins in the shoulders and the back of the neck, and dives with the same natural grace, as if for pearls. A coach spotted him nevertheless on one of our visits to the pool, and before he left London he had been taken up and given lessons and was winning medals for the local squad, where his wide-shouldered, muscular build, olive skin, and sheer God-given talent created frightful flutters of envy and lust among the pallid, much-coached middle-class children of whom the team was mostly composed.

Lessons, though, take the shine off a thing. So, all this winter, every weekend, skating. Ah, the inimitable whiff of the rink: socks, ammonia, and, right up the nose, that peculiar, chemical cold. The romance of the rink: the endless passeggiata of teenagers eyeing up each other's style; the 'ice-stewards' swinging around on their hockey skates like knights, rushing to the injured on one knee, shaved ice racking up behind them in a plume; the eighties power-ballads and licensed hand-holding; the outbursts of weird camp dancing. Ylli learned to skate on our first visit, simply by 'falling over thirty-two times' until his legs were black and blue. Now, he swooshes past us on the black-and-silver hockey skates I got him on eBay, plays tag with towering teenagers, indulges in proto-flirting with dolled-up eleven-year-olds, jumps, spins and – favourite trick – slo-mo runs on the ice – 'Catch me, Sam! Go on!' – grinning from ear to ear, blades clopping like a high-bred pony.

But first, we have to get there. It is only a couple of miles, but travelling with Ylli is never straightforward: there are circus tricks to be performed; Sam to be tended to and taught to skid on his little bike; passing dogs to be talked to; their owners to be charmed; and, most time-consuming of all, ducks. Ylli always gets overinvolved. A few weeks ago, he was disgusted by their mating behaviour, especially when one or two males were harassing a female. So ungallant. He stopped so often to abuse them, we lost nearly twenty minutes' rink time. On the other hand, he was also concerned by the groups of males who had given up the fight and were hanging out together instead:

'Kate – do you really get gay birds? Really?'

'Well, two male penguins reared an egg in New York Zoo, I heard.'

'Really? Was the little baby penguin gay?'

Ylli often exhausts my stores of information. He can be diverted, but only temporarily. I will have to return to the subject of whether being gay is heritable in penguins and in general all too soon, I can tell. Ylli is pretty liberal on the whole, but he is his mother's son when it comes to sexual mores and laundry. We have already been delayed this morning while he scraped mud from his new white tracksuit.

And today there is a new distraction: the ducklings are out, stripy and fluffy as bumblebees, six, seven, eight in a group, paddling earnestly in and out of the mud and weeds and rusting shopping trolleys. We have already stopped at least six times to exclaim over them, and when I see Ylli stooped yet again on the bank I am minded to proclaim seven too many. But there is no moving him. He has found a lost duckling, cheeping in lonesome circles behind a clump of weed.

'He wants his mum.'

'He does. He's got lost.'

'Well, where is she?'

'Up the canal somewhere.'

'How come she hasn't *noticed*?'

'Ylli, ducks can't count.'

'But she'd know he was *missing*.' Ylli has a husky little voice, deep for his age, with a catch to it. He has the huge, thickly fringed eyes of a colt or a child star. He has a trembling upper lip. When Flora and Ahmed were getting ready to leave Antigona's house for the last time, Ylli sat by me on a bench in the park and said, 'I don't want them to go. I don't want any one person more to go from my house. Seems like enough people have gone already.' Now, I know he is desperately worried about Mihane and her baby. He has texted her twice in the last half-hour. His feelings are simple: he wants them to come home. 'I don't mind about black and white, Kate,' he says, in a whisper, and when I affirm him, 'I don't actually care at all. I mean, my best friend at school, he's black, half-caste, mixed race, you know. Doesn't bother me, about the little baby.'

'Maybe the mother duck will come back,' I say, brightly. 'Or he might get picked up by another family – that happens quite a bit.'

'Or he might be killed by a fox.'

'Yeah.' I get off my bike. Ylli is leant over the bank, trying to open the reeds to make a little path for the duckling. Sam lies beside him, his small but passionately loyal lieutenant. There is no duck in sight. I can see we are in for a long wait.

When Jeannie's son got his bike taken by a bunch of eleven-year-old proto-hoodies, Ylli identified the criminals, and Antigona bearded them in London Fields. She told them they were disgraces to their mothers and their families. The boys started to give her a load of lip, but soon found themselves outgunned by rapid fire from a Kali-like incarnation of all things outraged and motherly. The strongest stood unmanned in the playground, open-mouthed, and the weakest dragged the bike from the rhododendrons.

'Why,' said Antigona later, genuinely baffled, 'are they like that? Taking a bike from a little boy? Saying fuck-you-this-and-that to me? Why doesn't their mums stop them?'

'They may not have mums.'

'Why doesn't the police stop them?'

'They've got too many other things to do. Besides, you can't lock up an eleven-year-old for stealing a bike.'

'Yeah, yeah, they go to court, they say social problems, single mum. Well, Ylli, he have harder time than anyone, and he never do that. He *hate* that.'

Ylli is ten now. He is the son of an alcoholic, a gambler and a wife-beater. He spent the first four years of his years in absolute poverty. He is a refugee and a victim of torture: held at gunpoint when he was two, nearly drowned when he was three, the veteran of three countries at four. He has been the witness of many horrible acts of violence and has known no reliable father figure. By the laws of statistics, genetics, and applied psychology, Ylli should be a juvenile criminal, a school dropout, a brandy-sipper, a bully or a desperate victim, a self-harming torturer of cats.

But Ylli is none of those things. He is the lodestar of his mother's life, gets into fights only when defending a victim, and is beloved of almost every life form in East London. He has learned to survive in his hostile landscape through the exercise of his charm. Like his mother, he swells almost visibly in company, bristling with cuteness like a baby owl, filling in any silence with a display of interest or athleticism. He can vault gates, one-handed. He can stand on his bike saddle while going downhill. I wish he wouldn't. Charm is how he got fed and attended to in a household where he was always much the smallest person, how he captured the attention of his errant father, how he kept himself safe with him, how he survived a drowning, a war. Now, no one can be exempt from noticing him: not tiny children, whom he kisses and hugs like his mother; not his teachers, whom he will quarrel with ruthlessly until they succumb and accord him special respect and the starring role in the school play; certainly not his peers, not one of them, from the cleverest, most middle-class girl in the class who always invites him to her birthday party, to the loutish boys Antigona drives from her door with shrieks. He climbed the school roof, one lunchtime. He is the best footballer in the school. There will be terrible trouble with girls in the future and several are lining up for his number already. His is the light that never goes out, and there is something draining about it, after a while: a hunger; an underlying, unappeasable anxiety.

Nevertheless. To concentrate on the overwhelmingly positive. Ylli is stooped over ducklings instead of holding up small boys for their bicycles outside Gayfield Primary. This is in itself a huge triumph over overwhelming odds. He has a strong sense of himself and a full hand of gifts and graces. He is perceptive well beyond his years: 'Aren't you tired?' he asks me. And,

'You have to stop worrying about Sam. It's not good for him.' He is remarkably without resentment, too. When he came to Sam's fourth birthday party he looked at the little boy poised over the cake with a knife, the golden head surrounded by parents, grandparents, cousins, and friends, and said, 'He doesn't know what to wish for. He's got everything already,' only a little wistfully. He must, I think, feel himself to be rich in love.

'Your nanny,' I have been told several times by mothers who have observed her at toddler group, 'is fantastic. She loves those children! Where did you get her?'

I am usually muted in my response. Partly, I suspect yet another shameless attempt to poach her. One woman actually proffered my wage in *cash* plus £50 for Saturdays, can you believe it? Partly, I know what they are talking about – Antigona's loud, passionate engagement with every toddler that passes, her extravagant, reckless affection for my children, her seizing of any baby and insistence on a smile – and find it a bit much, a little sentimental: ways, I suppose, of saying that it is so foreign to me that I cannot believe it is genuine. Mostly, though, I do know where it has come from, and am embarrassed by the reminder that, like so much else, I have bought this effusive affection for my children from abroad.

I am wary of childrearing books – Jean Liedloff's *The Continuum Concept* is perhaps the most famous – which advocate a return to 'primitive' childrearing practices as a cure for all Western ills. Such practices often seem to involve a wholesale sacrifice of the mother, for a start. Besides, I suspect that 'primitive' societies do contain depressed people and misfits (Liedloff notoriously thinks that sufficient hugging and lugging in the early years would eliminate, for example, homosexuality), though perhaps in ways which are not immediately obvious to the urban observer. Clearly, Kosovan villages did: Afrim, from Antigona's accounts, has suffered from depression for much of his life; Jehona has OCD; the KLA certainly contained sociopaths. Vendetta could be seen as a mass psychosis. And yet it is also clear to me that the life of the clan is right for little children: that they are happiest and learn most when they are with a group which includes a parent or other close adult alongside older and younger children, when they can join in a group activity and observe living things.

This is the life we have lost through industrialization, the life of the group and the life of the body: the life which nurseries try to recreate through 'stimulating activities', 'circle time' and 'nature tables', the life which 'play farms' and 'soft play centres' try to sell back to us, in the same way that city gyms have commoditized walking. 'I wouldn't like to have children here,' says Antigona. 'It is too hard. Here, you have to talk to them, play with them, and all these things.' Though, actually, Antigona talks to children all the time and likes nothing better than to join in their play. What she means is: here, childrearing is a self-conscious, pressured, rather lonely activity. She means, playing with children here has become a job, work, rather than a joyous break from it.

But we can't simulate the life of the clan, that elemental world of need and pressure, any more than we can really pretend there is nothing but soup for lunch. Children know there is something more in the cupboard. 'Children here have too many choices,' says Antigona. Too many toys, too many sorts of food: she thinks it makes them wasteful and quarrelsome. Besides, it takes the edge off presents, in which she has a child's delight. But something of the life of the clan was Antigona's gift to my children. Everywhere she went with them – and they went everywhere, in every weather – Antigona drew groups of women and children around her. My children learnt from her to participate and relax in a group in a way that I, the compulsive observer, never could.

When Antigona is with small children, and especially if she is outside, in natural surroundings, she is full of unstinting, infectious joy. She would walk the children for hours, you feel, the youngest on her back, the next in size holding her hands, and they would walk with her. She loves to feed them, smiling as each bite goes down, and to wash them, and see their faces shine. This is the easiest, best bit of your life, her gestures say, who would miss this? To have enough food to give your child, to dress your baby skin-out in fresh clothes – oh, what lucky spot of time have we arrived at, what patch of sun in the woods! What could be better, now, than to sit down and pass the little one from hand to hand and say – begging the Evil Eye's pardon – that surely he is the loveliest baby ever seen?

Antigona knows what children cost. She aborted six, in horrible, amateur abortions which she can hardly bear to speak about, in order to save herself from what she knew would be intolerable poverty and labour. Yet she still thinks babies are the greatest joy in life. She decided to have Ylli because it would give her joy to love him, not to fill his father's heart with pride. When Mihane was missing, I would tell Antigona it would come right. 'You gave her all that love when she was little. At the bottom of her heart, in her real self, she still has that. And in the end, she will come back to you.' It was the only thing that could stop her crying. She knew it was true: she knew she had given her very best.

Women here, I think, are too prone to treat the early years of a child's life as a 'problem', something to get over as soon as possible. In the Albanian *fis*, those early years were a woman's great compensation, the point of her life. So great a joy, in fact, that it was forbidden to speak of it: in her first years here, Antigona would shush me, fearfully, forcefully, if I rejoiced in my children, if I said how sweet Sam looked in a new shirt. I would make other women envious, she said, and they would bring down the Evil Eye. When Sam developed a stammer she blamed the Evil Eye, and me, for persistently delighting in his chatter. Pride in your children should be kept close in your heart, like the deepest romances, like an affair.

Antigona desperately needed more choices in her life

than just mothering, and so, surely, did many of her peers. But here we often exclude women from choosing mothering, even for a short time. I am suspicious of Madonna-worship – of the exultation of mother and child – as I am suspicious of Antigona's gush about children, on feminist grounds, thinking it to be a cover for a narrowing of choices such as Antigona has suffered, or for misogyny, the hatred of all women who are not mothers. But my years with Antigona make me think that perhaps I am too English, too chilly, too narrow and, perhaps, not feminist enough: after all, only women have this, these early years of mother with baby, this particular trial and romance. Why should we never mention it, or deny it is one of the grand loves of our lives?

'There were three brothers, and they were building a big building, like a castle? – A church? But not.'

Usually I have to prompt Antigona to tell folk tales, but today there is one on her mind. I notice *Take A Break* magazine, in her bag: a feature on battered wives. 'A temple?' I suggest.

'OK. A temple. And every day they built it, and every night the building fell down. So they went to – you know – like the Imam, but not. A thing that say the future. What is going to happen.'

'The oracle?'

'OK. Oracle. And the oracle say to the brothers, "You need to kill someone. You made a mistake. You didn't say your prayers when you start to build the temple – so now you have to kill someone and bury them under the walls." So the brothers discuss, and they decide, whichever wife come tomorrow with the lunch, we will bury her. And they agree, we will not tell the wives, fair contest. But that night, two of the brothers they tell their wives, don't come with the lunch, but the youngest, he is straight, he doesn't tell.

'And the next day, the mother-in-law say, "Who will take the lunch to the work," and the oldest wife say she is ill, and the next one, she says her child is ill, and the youngest one, she have a baby, just nine months, feeding at her breast, and she say, "OK, I will take the lunch, but you take my baby."

'And then she went up to the place and the brothers say, "Now you have to die." And she is brave. She say, "OK, bury me, but leave out one eye, and one arm, and one ear and one breast. Because I need to see my baby and hear him and feed him and give him a cuddle." And so they do. And her eye keeps seeing the baby, and her ear keeps hearing him, and her arm give him a cuddle, and her breast keeps giving out milk, even though the rest of her is stone.'

It is the story of a sacred spring. 'There is still milk there, still coming from the stone,' says Antigona. 'Still there. Or maybe not now. But recently. Before the war.'

To give out all this love, to harbour these deep contents, Antigona herself must have been well mothered. Fatmire was fourteen when she was married off, as a strong peasant girl, to the depressive and least promising son of a well-off family. Her mother-in-law sat her below the salt and fed her whey when the other daughters-in-law had curds: she bore Blerta when she was just fifteen years old. Her terrible illness and the death of the golden baby occurred before she was thirty. But that fourteen-year-old girl must have been full of strength and faith and love; she must have been old enough to give her offspring strong, secure babyhoods and childhoods. All Fatmire's children thrived; all of them grew up survivors. Blerta, Vera, Agim, Driton: each has held steady through war, bereavement and disaster; not one of them has ever given up, and that takes more than a strong work ethic. Fatmire's children have survived torture. When I think of Jehona, I remember the famous photograph from the Kosovan War of a woman who has hanged herself from a tree: this Jehona did not do, so she must have a core of self-worth that could not be violated. Even Hasan, who I thought was a lost cause, has survived his depression to become a changed man. And Antigona, the strongest of them all, has passed through fire, water and her own most deeply held prejudices into an entirely new world.

Because in the end, Antigona's love will be stronger even than the Kanun of Lek. She is on the turn: already she says of the new baby, her grandchild, 'He has done nothing wrong. He is angel. He is child.'

'I want to be in Albania now,' says Ylli, when we finally get going again (I have no certain news, fellow animal-lovers, on the duckling. It disappeared, despite our best efforts, into the reeds). 'Mum doesn't want to, but I do.'

'Your mum's worried about your future.'

'She shouldn't worry. I like it there. If I was there, I could have a dog.'

'Who has dogs there?'

'My uncle. Vera's husband. Like massive, massive dogs, bigger than Sam, easily, for hunting.'

'Boarhounds.'

'Probably. And horses. Oh, man, I'd love a horse. I'd love a donkey, even. Or even like – you know, a donkey-horse thing—'

'A mule.'

'Yeah. They kick, though. And there's a lake there, too, in Albania.'

'At your grandma's house?'

'Yeah – like right outside the back garden. You can dive in, go swimming – nobody there!'

When Ylli and Antigona came back from their Albanian holiday, they both, separately, told me the same story. On their way home through Tirana, Ylli needed a pee, so Antigona took him to a cafe and bought him a lemonade as the price of the facilities. Ylli loves Sprite, but this drink turned out to be an Albanian lookalike, and Ylli wanted no more than a sip of it. There was a barefoot boy in the road outside, a wound on his knee wrapped in a plastic bag. 'Give the drink to him,' said Antigona, but Ylli refused. 'He wouldn't want it, Mum, I've drunk some!'

'He would,' said Antigona, and Ylli went out. The boy was probably his contemporary but he was a head shorter. Ylli held out the drink. The boy looked him up and down, then grabbed it and gulped. Then he choked, recovered, wiped his nose, kept drinking.

'He hadn't had a fizzy drink before,' said Ylli to me. 'Even though he lived right there, by the cafe.'

'I wanted Ylli to see what he could be, there,' says Antigona. 'How lucky he is.'

Ahead of Ylli, I see the ways dividing. On the one hand, the littered Hackney towpath, with its exuberant wild flowers and silent fishermen and outcrops of unidentifiable stinking rubbish. What is through that long brick arch that leads west, into London? Football stardom, Ylli is convinced. The army, he says on other days, until I remind him he might have to kill someone. Lifeguarding, I think optimistically, youth work. And many, many worse fates for handsome immigrant boys from broken homes with romantic, questing dispositions.

On Ylli's other hand, Albania. There, his mother sees that barefoot boy with the wounded knee and raw skin round the eyes and nose, the half-made, crazy streets of Tirana. She thinks of Vera's son who walked to Greece twice to find work as a shepherd, and was arrested and beaten up by the border guard for his trouble, of her fifteen-year-old cousin whom she has just helped apprentice to a double-glazing factory for £15 a week. Ylli, though, is imagining a blue lake and a green lane, an ancient, cobbled mule-path through the forest. The life of the body, the harsh, beautiful horseman's life he was born to, the life of men.

I'm not sure it's there. The life of the *fis* which

survived wars and communism is changing now under the more subtle and overwhelming forces of globalization, television, and migration. Many families of the Malësi are headed by women now, as their men go abroad, or as their women come back, changed by what they have seen in Italy or England. Talk talk, go the mobile phones, and an hour's cleaning in England can bring in more food than a week's hunting in the diminishing forest. Vera's husband is one of the last of his kind, which is one reason why he is so angry. Ylli had better stay here.

FREEDOM

'When I come back to England,' said Antigona after her long holiday in Albania, 'I kiss the ground. Because here I am free.' I knew she had loved the time with her mother and sisters, the fresh food, the clean air, so I asked her what she meant. 'Free to get money,' she said.

And I know that is important. Earning her own money and being allowed to keep it and save it is a key to Antigona's changed status in the eyes of her family and to the growth of her own self-esteem. It allows her to work purposefully, to keep her children, to provide for herself. It is indivisible from her freedom, not, as the term 'economic migrant' might suggest, a separate issue. But there is more:

'Free from opinion. Free from people talking behind your back.'

'Free from shame?'

'Yeah. No.' Antigona wants to make the full statement. She may never get the chance to take our multiple-choice citizenship test, but she is showing me she has a full appreciation of the civil society.

'Free to walk on the street, no one will hurt you. Anyone does anything, you call the police, and the police are fair. Free to be in my house – shut the door. Free to do my life how I want it. This is important thing. Free to choose.'

After the rink, with our legs aching in the strange muscles skating pulls at, we get back on the bikes.

'No ducks, OK?' I say to Ylli, as we push down to the canal.

'I just want to see if that little lost one's all right.'

'The duckling? How are you going to recognize him?'

But Ylli is away, and when, two turns of the path later, Sam and I catch up with him again, he is feeding a troop of swans. Someone has given him a bag of bread. He is deep in conversation with the presumed donor – a fat old man with thick glasses and a terrible track suit. Ah. An Odd Bod.

Odd Bods are another hazard of travelling with Ylli. They want to talk to him, especially the men. He reminds them of something. They have something for him. We have never been to London Fields without spending at least half an hour talking to a old man about a dog he remembers, in Poland or in Italy, a dog he really liked, and who liked him; never cycled down the towpath without at least one reminiscence of someone's first bike, and how they too, used to scare their mum with their tricks. 'Look, Mum, no hands. Look Mum, no feet. Look, Mum, no teeth.' We are connoisseurs of the phlegmy laugh and the toothless whoop. Ylli collects tips, quite often, and tells them his name, and how it means 'luck', and then they can shout, 'Good luck, Lucky' after him, and have that to chew on all day, the name and the quip, the thought of the coin in the pocket, the memory of a boy at one with his bike.

And I'm tolerant, on the whole. It's a good thing, I tell myself, to bring the village with you in this way. Good for Sam, who is already so stiff and so English. But today, I am exhausted with ducklings and starving for my lunch. I am exhausted with Antigona, too, the row about Mihane, this new thing about the papers – really, it has taken all My Time for the last week. I get off my bike and advance with my chilliest, most middle-class, most Teflon smile.

But this Odd Bod knows about swans, at least. Ylli's bag contains grain, not bread, and the Odd Bod is teaching him to hold the wheat flat on his hand, and have the swan peck it off. 'They won't do you any harm,' he says, nodding to me. 'Last year's cygnets, see the pale beaks? And some grey feathers still there, too. Couldn't find any lady swan that would have them, so here they are. Just a bunch of lads. Up from Victoria Park for the day.' And he laughs a wheezy laugh. The swans bend their heads to the water, docile, abashed. Ylli kneels on the bank and empties out the last grain in the bag. We all pause, wanting the moment to last.

'I saw a swan die, once,' the old man says then.

'Die?' says Ylli. 'How did you know?'

'You know what he did? He flew up, straight up in the air, high as he could go; three hundred feet, then he plummeted down into the water.'

'Is that true?' says Ylli.

'True as I stand here,' says the old man, and we all look at his outsize white trainers.

'That's what they do. They know it's coming.'

And then we bike back, our minds free of premonition. Ylli comes in for lunch as usual, munches salad with his elbows out, cuts himself great hunks of bread. Then he says he has got to go to football practice up on the Marshes. He joined a Boys' League team last year, and I can see that soon it will overtake even swimming in his passions. We make no special fuss about saying goodbye, because we have no idea that we will never see him again. Six days later, he will be in Croydon, in a shopping centre, holding his nephew in his arms while a reconciliation begins awkwardly over their beloved heads. Eight days later, he will be in a Detention Centre, awaiting deportation; ten days later, on a plane.

When he phones us on his last night, he tells me to look out for the lost duckling next Sunday, because he feels bad we never found its mum. Then he says he should be in school; it seems all wrong, this place. And he tells me I must say to his football team and to his coach and to his teacher and to Sam the very first word he learnt in English: 'Sorry.' I promise him I will, and I do.

EPILOGUE

Flora's CV

September 2007

Flora has come round. We are sitting in my office giggling at her old CV, the one we strenuously padded out to get her into college. She has her headscarf off, since it's just me. Her hair is bobbed – 'like Posh Spice', she says, but it curls prettily round her head instead of falling sternly over one eyebrow. She has dropped the burka, too, in general, and returned to dress-over-trousers ensembles. Today, she is elegant in black and white swirls from Top Shop. She has vowed never to enter Miss Selfridge again.

'We did a great job on this,' I say, looking at the crumpled paper. 'I especially like the way it goes straight from 2002 to 2004 without mentioning why.'

'I should just have written: Nervous Breakdown, 2003; Graduated, 2004,' says Flora, a little bitterly.

'Oh, come on,' I say. 'Look at the rest of it. Primary education, Kosovo – then two years doing . . . What, exactly?'

'Housework. Two years' housework.'

'Right. Then torture, shop in Italy, followed by the

most terrifying school in all of Hackney – if you hadn't had a nervous breakdown, it would be worrying. Honestly. Cut yourself some slack. Look how well you're doing now.'

For the last fourteen months, Flora has been working for the same solicitors who handled her own and her mother's immigration cases. She has been flourishing: officially there to file and answer phones, she seems to spend at least half of her time interpreting for clients: Albanians, Italians, and Kurds. I've been urging her to study to be a paralegal, or to interpret for the police, at the very least. She loves her languages. She loves the law.

'Remember,' she tells me, pointing at the manuscript on my floor, 'you can't write anything about Mum's case in that book. Or Ylli's. It's *sub judice*.'

'I know, Flora. I'll remember.'

'When I'm not here to keep an eye on you.'

'I'm not going to say anything about it at all. I promise.'

Ahmed has been doing well in the last year, too, working for an uncle back in Mosul. 'Import–Export,' says Flora, grandly, but I can never work out of what, exactly. Something that earns enough for Ahmed to have suits, anyway, and a car, and now the chance to do 'Import–Export' back in the family home in Germany. Flora is going, too. I wish she wouldn't.

'I have to go with my husband,' says Flora proudly. And Ahmed has proved to be an excellent husband in the recent adversity: loyal, kind, and the holder of an impeccable set of EU papers. They still fight, though: probably, they always will.

There will be a clan waiting for Flora in Germany, a Kurdish clan that already bombard her with photos and phone calls and gifts. There will be a women's quarters for her to settle in, drink coffee, giggle. And she has little enough family here. Driton has moved with Maria to Spain, where he has a job with his father-in-law's construction firm. Hasan was labouring on alone in London and sending money to his family, but this year he has not returned from his summer break in Albania. It's the air, he tells Antigona on the phone, the food, the quality of his sleep. He can't bear to go back to London, he can't bear to leave his mother's house.

So that leaves Mihane. The girls are reconciled: they speak on the phone most weeks, they visit each other at least once a month. Flora is an affectionate aunt, and Ahmed an outstanding babysitter, but, like the good Kosovan girls they are at heart, Antigona's daughters are both part of their husband's clans now. Mihane got married, like Flora, in the papers flurry, but it is only her mother-in-law she speaks of. She has her own flat, but leaves her child with his grandmother most days while she attends her college course. She is doing accounts. On the phone, she sounds more than ever like a black girl from Croydon. 'How's ya breeder?' she asks Flora of Ahmed, irritating her extremely, and 'Yeah, yeah, cool, cool,' whenever I try to probe a little deeper.

'I'll lose touch with Mihane, if you go,' I complain to Flora. 'You know how she's always changing her number.'

'Mum'll give it to you,' says Flora. 'She always phones mum, in the end.' And it's true: she does.

Antigona is close with both her daughters again, and I too have joined the circle of female relatives on the other end of her mobile, being shouted at and periodically disconnected as Antigona pushes a Bugaboo pushchair round a new set of swings, in a new (cleaner and tidier, apparently) park, with statues, in another European city.

'You'll be able to visit your mum, from Germany,' I suggest, hopefully. 'It's only a day on the train.'

'If she can get the time off, ' says Flora, because there isn't much time off in Antigona's new job. And we pause to giggle a little, as we always do, about Antigona's pompous new employers.

'Well, so long as they pay her,' I say, feeling my familiar ache of worry about Antigona, the tug of responsibility about her legality and her papers.

'They'll pay her,' says Flora, rising to go. I open the door for her and the golden autumnal sun streams in. We blink in it, smiling.

'Come on,' says Flora. 'You know my mum.'

I look at the manuscript on my floor. It asks me, 'And what do you know?' a thousand times a day. Then I think of Antigona, smiling at me as we sat on the wall in my street, watching our little boys play; Antigona in the playground, turning to me in delighted surprise as I came puffing over with some forgotten item – a coat, clean trousers – and pointing out the children, outrageously high on the slide; Antigona in my kitchen, hands full of washing, telling me something extraordinary and terrible about her life.

'Yes,' I say. 'Yes, of course. I mean, I hope so.'

Select Bibliography

I found these books, reports, and websites especially useful when I was writing this book, and have cited some of them:

Cox, Rosie, *The Servant Problem: Domestic Employment in a Global Economy* (I. B. Tauris, 2006)

Durham, Edith, *High Albania* (Virago, 1908)

Greer, Germaine, *The Female Eunuch* (Flamingo Modern Classics, 1970)

Friedan, Betty, *The Feminine Mystique* (Penguin, 1963)

Judah, Tim, *Kosovo: War and Revenge* (Yale Note Bene, 2002)

Malcolm, Noel, *Kosovo: A Short History* (Macmillan, 1998)

Seierstad, Asne, *With Their Backs to the World: Portraits from Serbia* (Virago, 2002)

Wolf, Naomi, *Misconceptions* (Chatto and Windus, 2001)

A Week of Terror in Drenica: Humanitarian Law Violations in Kosovo Human Rights Watch, 1999

Domestics: UK Domestic Workers and their Reluctant Employers The Work Foundation, 2004

Lala Meredith Vula–arresting photographs of Kosovo and of refugees:
http://lalameredithvula.com/images
Human Rights Watch:
http://www.hrw.org
UNHCR – The UN Refugee Agency:
http://www.unhcr.org
UNHCR statistics:
http://www.unhcr.org/statistics
BBC News Kosovo fact files:
http://www.news.bbc.co.uk/hi/english/static/kosovo_fact_files/default.stm
BBC News special report, 1998, Kosovo:
http://www.news.bbc.co.uk/1/hi/special_report/1998/kosovo/default.stm

Acknowledgements

Matthew Reynolds, Joanna Rabiger, Charlotte Greig, Caroline Warman and Monique Roffey all gave me generous and helpful readings of this text as it evolved. Matthew Reynolds, Margaret Reynolds, Joan Clanchy and Michael Clanchy worked to give me the time I needed to solve my 'Problem' and get to my desk. Flora's candid confidence in me, and her willingness to allow me to portray her honestly through the huge changes of adolescence, reflect her generous and brave character. My great debt to Antigona herself is, I hope, recorded in the preceding pages: I will continue to pay it.

OXFAM has been working in Albania since 1992, giving support to poor mountain communities. Local organizations and local rural people work with us, developing innovative ways for people to make a secure living; and helping producers to improve production and to reach markets. Such initiatives help to create new jobs within a community. More widely, Oxfam is campaigning with and for small farmers on local producers and for the needs to develop the rural economy.

To donate to Oxfam's work in Albania please go to www.oxfam.org.uk/albania or call 0300 200 1300.